Were Only Married in the Bed

By: Brian Carline

PRESS

Table of Contents

Dedication

I dedicate this book first to Jesus Christ for laying down His life for me and for others on the cross.

Secondly, I dedicate this work to my wife, Evangelist Yvonne Carline. Thank you for your spiritual support, prayers, words of encouragement, and your investments.

I would like to dedicate this to my children, grandchildren, brothers, sisters, aunts and uncles. Also, thanks to my past, present, and future coworkers. Thank you to my pastor Evangelist Christy Edgar and my Gospel brothers and sisters, Gospel sons, daughters, and grandchildren.

Last but not least, a very special thanks to my business associates for their support, assistance, and talents. Thank you to my Gospel daughter and executive assistant, Tiffany Benson. Thanks to Mr. Paul Johnson for the book cover and art work.

Look for *A Slave to Love Volume 2 (2010-2011)
*I Do Volume 3 (late 2012)

We have all been created for a purpose. We have been given special talents and abilities. It is very important for you to know your purpose in this world. Sometimes we transform into other people and we succumb to the wrong purposes. Deep down there is a void that will never be filled.

I pray that after you read this book the scales will fall completely off your eyes. I pray for you to see the truth about your life and your purpose. I pray that for the rest of your lifetime people will no longer be able to use you, manipulate you, or play games with your mind.

I will see you at the end of this book...

INTRODUCTION

There are sounds of a baby crying....
A mother stares into the eyes of her beautiful baby girl...

Instantly, she flashes back to the times in her life where she made mistakes and never thought twice about her choices. Now, after finding out the truth, she's unsure of how she can use wisdom to guide her little girl into the world controlled by evil desires...

Another mother stares into the eyes of her handsome baby boy...

With all the battle scars from being involved with men, she's wondering in the back of her mind if she can help nurture her son. Her heart is racing as she stares into her son's eye—and she can see through his eyes the man that caused her pain.

Life—
We have no way to see or
predict the future...

Meet the fellas...

Joe > He is the sexy, good looking guy who works as a stripper...

Darryl > A school bus driver, heavy stomach, loves to watch television, eat, and sleep...

Kevin > Successful lawyer with no conscience, a control freak—*his way or no way*...

Mark > He is the local dog with seven flea girlfriends...

Peter > Always physically fighting with his wife, always plays the "blame game", never completes anything he starts...

Brad > This is the liar from hell, has *never* told the truth from the time he was conceived...

James > A dreamer who *always* talks...about nothing...

Now, meet the ladies...

Lora > Works as a Las Vegas call girl...

Lorraine > She's a doctor who never has time for husband, she has no children...

Susan > Husband stealer...

Stacy > Is always crying and feeling sorry for herself...

Donna > Insecure, no confidence, never seems to know her hair style—*the wig or weave?*...

Karen > Always angry, she hates everyone...

Kathy > She is the former high school cheer-leader who lives in a fantasy world, 40-years-old and still a cheerleader looking for Mr. Right...

CHAPTER 1

We move too fast

Most people meet in life to either love or hurt others. At the age of Sweet-16, from television, magazines—we fantasize of marrying a rich and famous spouse. But overnight, we end up with a dead end job...

Darryl is sitting on the couch right now watching television. He has not a care in the world other than his remote and his love for football...

Stacy can't seem to stop crying because she never had the perfect wedding. Everything in her life has gone wrong since the day she said "I do"...

We carry so much of our past into the future that we forget how to live day to day. We are blinded by our past hurt. Oh, my god! Mom and dad never took time to teach us how to forgive the people who hurt us the most. So we continue to make bad choices and marry the wrong person. Before you can ever love the new person in your life, you must learn to forgive and let go all personal feelings and mistakes... If you can do that, then you can be free.

*Now, look at **Joe** — sexy, very good looking...and you keep saying in the back of your mind, "Maybe, just maybe, I can control Joe. I can make him love me and stop being a stripper."*

*And look at **Lora** — I just gave her $1000 to forget about my wife and my bad kids at home...for just one hour...*

You are still in love with your ex and can't move on because life has you at a standstill. You've lied to yourself and convinced yourself that it was over. And your friends — so-called friends — didn't have the heart to tell you the truth. You continue to go on blind dates, thinking you are ready to move on.

Remember when you hooked up with **Mark**? He had you thinking you were the only one. You forgot about **Peter**. He made all those promises with no intentions of fulfilling them...Oh! And **Brad** — he made excuses for every day. Do not forget, **Brad** is the liar from hell!

It's common nature for men and women to become desperately lonely — so lonely that they fall in love with those on soap operas. You dress for attention and every time — the wrong one shows up. It's almost like going to the doctor and he gives you medicine, but you only take it until you start feeling better. Your body tricks you into thinking that the problems are gone. It creates an illusion so that you stop taking you medicine.

Meeting new people in our lives, we try to hide the truth of who we really are by having fun. Sometimes we often convince ourselves that by "moving on" the hurt *will* stop! You are only tricking yourself and others when you think this way. But you go on, having a fairy tale relationship for three to twelve months, and then you get married. And after all the wedding guests have gone home...the band has played the last song...last kiss from a family member...we go on this extraordinary honeymoon, but on our way to the airport we realize—*we have nothing in common.* So now, you have just played with another person's life...

Life

Look at **Mark**—He's got seven girlfriends! Seven. A different girl for every day of the week...

Look at **Susan**—she's riding in the car with your man...after he just got paid...

Let's not forget about **Kathy**—still thinking she's a cheerleader...has had more men than the days of the month-and still not married...

Darryl—has more fun watching football on Sunday than talking to you...

Slow down **Lorraine**! Slow down!—I was hoping, Honey, we could have dinner...you haven't made it home early one night this week!

Karen—why do you have me so much? What have I done to you?

One day you wake up, you look at high school scrap books and recognize you've wasted thirty years of your life because you move to fast. And who do you blame? Do you blame **Joe, Darryl, Kevin, Mark, Peter, Brad, James**? You ask, "Why me?"... Its all **Lora, Lorraine, Susan, Stacy, Donna, Karen, and Kathy's** fault...

Oops! Rewind! The world was created in seven days, so how do you expect to build a marriage to last a lifetime? Hmm...just about now you're asking yourself, how do I do that? Most people in the world build their marriage with straws—the first storm will blow that marriage down. Some people try to build with concrete, but in time it begins to crack...or you can build a marriage to last a lifetime—build it with steal, coat it with copper...Don't get scared...there you go again...your mind is racing...you're thinking... thinking about all the marriages you've personally seen go through countless divorce. It's not an easy formula to pick the right mate.

For instance, take **Kevin**...hmm...**Kevin**—he's a ruthless lawyer...And think about **Kathy**—the woman has been a cheerleader for forty years...One day, **Kevin** is going through the subway, looks to his right and there stands **Kathy**—Miss Cheerleader. He stares into her eyes and she stares back into his. But the first thing **Kevin** notices is she's dressed as a marketable product. She's trying to sell herself based on her outer appearance.

Freeze!

Now, I want you to take a moment and put yourself in this scene...And all of a sudden you believe you've found Mr. or Mrs. Right. You exchange numbers and arrange to go on this date. Both of you exit the subway with warm smiles and pleasant greetings.

"Oh! Girl! You have no idea who I met today! I met my future baby daddy! "..."Girl, let me tell you... can you imagine...tall, Denzel, and the eyes of **Brad**... Mmm!"... "I looked at his hand—I saw no ring! We exchanged numbers and made arrangements to go to lunch. Did you hear me! Girl! You see what I got on! He couldn't take his eyes off me!"

"Good afternoon, **Susan**."

"Good afternoon, **Kevin**."

"Do you have any messages for me?...Hey, **James**, come here for a minute!"

"How you doing, **Kevin**?"

"Aw, man...just about to add a new trophy to my case."

"A new trophy?"

"Yeah...some bimbo on the subway, still thinking she's a cheerleader. I just let her talk...talk...and talk... but I was only thinking about one thing."..."Okay, James, I'll talk to you later..."

Ding Dong! Ding Dong!

"Just a minute!...Oh, hi, **Kevin**!"

"Hi, **Kathy**."

"Thank you for such beautiful flowers! Give me a moment to put these in a vase and we'll be on our way!"

As she began to walk off with the flowers, **Kevin** commented to himself, *the way she's dressed, I'll have this trophy in my case sooner than I thought."*

They walk outside into a cool, breezy evening. **Kevin** –being such a gentlemen—he opens her door. When she gets into the car she notices another beautiful rose on the seat. She picks it up before she sits down and looks at **Kevin** and says, "Why?"

"Because something good just happened to me."

They begin to approach the freeway and **Kevin**'s just listening to her talk...and listening to her talk...and he always responds in such a way that she would continue to talk...
As they begin to have dinner, **Kevin** talks about college days...the firm he's working for...the fraternity he participated in...

Sitting about seven tables away, a group of young ladies are also having dinner. A certain young lady makes eye contact with **Kevin**. And **Kevin** makes eye contact with her...**Kathy** noticed the interaction between them, and he responded,

"That may be a former client of mine."

So they continue to have dinner...laugh...joke, jester...**Kevin** excuses himself to go to the men's room. Across the way, the young lady noticed him move. As **Kevin** approached the men's room, she approached the ladies' room...she slipped him a piece of paper.

Kevin exited the restaurant and continues his good evening with **Kathy** — the bimbo. **Kevin** begins to tell her of his dreams of one day having a beautiful family to love and nurture...maybe one day his son or daughter can take over his practice. Immediately, **Kathy** began to put herself in that role of his wife...

Kevin just drove around the city...listening to beautiful music. He stops by the law firm, takes her to the hundredth floor and allows her to look out of his office window. She saw the beautiful city of lights below...she *instantly* forgot about all the lies and games men had played with her and all the scars from past relationships...

"Oh my god! Its seven o'clock! **Kevin**, wake up! I got to go to work!"

She wakes **Kevin** up. He gets out of bed and begins to get dressed...and with a devilish look he tells her, "I'll see you around."

She lies quietly in the bed, feeling embarrassed, feeling shamed, and feeling dirty. **Kevin** slowly walks out of the house and as he drives off he says to himself, *just another hoe...*

Kathy quietly stays there, just paralyzed, thinking about what she'd just done. She gets up slowly...she walks to the shower. As the water begins to fall on her face, tears begin to stream out of both eyes. She slowly steps out of the shower, tears still falling, and she decides not to go to work.

As the day progresses, she decides to give **Kevin** a call. His secretary answers—who is **Susan**—puts her on hold, comes back to the line, "May I take a message? He's not available."

Kathy makes several attempts to contact **Kevin** with no luck.

Freeze this frame!

In life, most people, on their first date, normally put on a big mask. It's not really who these persons are. Your first date should be a date of truth.

Chapter 2

Gold Diggers

"Your Honor, I refuse to pay child support. This is absurd! $1500 a month! She was never worth me marrying!"

Your fault!

One night, **Lorraine** decides to hang out with **Joe**. They go on a date and she noticed all the ladies knew **Joe**. From the left, "Hi, Joe!" From the right, "Hi, Joe!" Even the waitress, "Hi, Joe!" As the evening got late Lorraine's pager went off; an emergency call from the hospital. She looks into Joe's eyes and says,

"**Joe**, I must go to the hospital."

Joe gladly responds with a big smile, "Okay, **Lorraine**, I'll see you later."

Before the valet brought **Lorraine's** car forward, Joe was heading to the bar. He sat there for five minutes and **Susan** asks to buy him a drink. **Joe** responds,

"Thank you kindly."

Silence...

Joe tries to feel guilty because he just had a wonderful evening with **Lorraine**. All of a sudden he gets a text from **Lorraine** saying, *"I'll see you tomorrow. I had a wonderful evening."* **Joe** blushed, looked over and told **Susan**,

"That was just a friend reminding me of something."

Joe began to strike up interesting conversation that leads up to Central Park. He began to tell **Susan** his wonderful dream that one day he's going to retire and buy a little white house with a white picket fence somewhere outside the city. And he also told her about the wonderful kids he hoped to raise.

You are so stupid if you believe that line!

Most men and women try to recover from past hurts and memories by moving into a new relationship—without completely being healed in the mind, body, and soul. It's in our nature for a man to be attracted to a woman, and a woman attracted to a man. So we must learn to take the proper time in laying a foundation for a marriage that's going to last a lifetime.

We spend hours shopping for homes, cars, clothes, hairstylists, barbers, jobs...but we only invest a *few dates* to determine whether or not to spend a lifetime with our future mate! A light bulb should have flashed on! If you buy a car—they ask for references. If you get a job—they ask for references. If you buy a home—they ask for paperwork. So why don't you take these five suggestions the next time you go on a date:

- *Names and numbers of the last three relationships—your references.*
- *Ask to see or have a copy of divorce papers.*
- *Is it okay if I come by* work *and have lunch with you?*
- *Do you believe in God and Jesus?*
- *When was the last time you had sex?*

Looking at television one night, you recognize how people live beautiful lives. They have nice homes, nice **cars, and the perfect marriage. But do you ever take time to realize these are paid actors and actresses on a** television show? These shows are designed to sell ratings. It is merely entertainment; advertising executives being approached by television networks and executive producers of a show designed to make money. So now you've built your fantasy world based on a made up world. This is because you have never been taught to deal with reality. About this time you're ready to put this book down—don't do it!

Don't do it!

Just for sake of argument think about **Kathy**—our 40-year-old cheerleader, who's never stopped being a cheerleader...or think about **Lora**—our Las Vegas Call Girl (but she's really a hoe)...And what about **Joe**? **Joe** goes to the health club every day just to be buff. **Joe** capitalizes on weak, silly women that fantasize about having a buff man...Every Thursday night—Ladies' Night—**Joe** knows hundreds of women are coming to the club so he can fulfill their fantasies. They begin to drink, *pretend* to be happy, and give away a whole day's pay in tips to **Joe**...and all so they can feel good about themselves.

I hear you breathing hard now...I hear you breathing...why you sweating? Hold this thought for a moment. Let me give you my definition of a female gold-digger...and my definition of a male gold-digger:

A gold-digger is the son or daughter of the devil, because the devil is the father and creator of lies and illusions.

Listen! Didn't you hear that voice telling you not to get involved? But somehow or another your mind pulled forth your perfect soul mate. All your life you've searched to meet Mr. and Mrs. Right.

Subconsciously you've created a person that does not exist. And a gold-digger finds a way to temporarily fill this void in your life until you don't have a penny left to your name. Let's identify a gold-digger:

- shops only at expensive stores
- spends more time at health clubs than a job
- joins the most high net worth country club in their area
- charges up major credit cards
- leases expensive cars (Jaguar, Beamer, Mercedes, etc...)

You ever had that thought in the back of your mind that somebody's watching you? Well, a gold-digger spends weeks, months, years—depending on the reward, or your financial net worth.

Just a minute! Just a minute! Take the time to pull yourself together! Get up, walk around...okay calm down...don't kill 'em—hold on! Because you might be someone's gold-digger. So, life presents difficult and unexpected situations.

Let's talk about **James** for a moment...**James** is a dreamer, but on the other side he's a gold-digger... or **Karen**—she hates everybody...

Karen was getting ready to buy a new boat. She calls her banker on the phone and her banker advised, "Sure, **Karen**, would you like that to be in you and your husband's name—**James**?"

Few minutes later, he calls **Karen** back with disturbing news. He tells her **James** is broke, bad credit, and has filed bankruptcy. So he advised **Karen** to put the boat in her name only.

"Hmm..." **Karen**'s saying.

She realizes all the information **James** told her about his finances are all lies. She gets up from her desk—furious, angry, and upset with herself. Then she said to herself,

"Now, everything makes sense...I co-signed for him to get a new car, lent him money he never paid me back...I invested in his so-called company that he needed $10,000 in start up capital...Mmm...and it was so strange he asked me to sign a new one million dollar life insurance policy three days after we got married. But I was so blind to my perfect man, I couldn't see beyond the missing void in my life— that he filled so perfectly."

Karen paced up and down the floor that day, practicing on how to confront all his lies—*uh-oh! There he is! Nice new Corvette that I co-signed for him to get...*
Karen walked over to the wine cabinet and fixed a glass just to settle her nerves. Don't you know he had nerve to come through the door with a dozen roses and this perfectly wrapped little box? He greeted **Kathy** with such a smile and a gentile touch.

"Hi, Honey! I just couldn't get you off my mind. These flowers remind me of the joy, peace, and happiness you bring me. And this is a little gift of many to come for all the support you have given me."

Instantly, **Karen**'s heart began to race, tears began to run down her face... **James** continued to fill that void she'd searched for all of her life. And at that moment, because of the love she had for him, she chose to accept a lie over the truth.

"Honeybun! Honeybun, I'm gonna take a quick shower. Then I'm going to take you to the restaurant where we first met."

Reality Check!

Often in life we suppress the truth with a lie. It's easier to close our eyes to the truth than to deal with it. Seventy-five percent of marriages are built on lies with very little truth. Marriages built on the truth have a lifetime expectancy of ten to fifty years. If you had a choice would you marry someone for a few months or for fifty years? Somebody just asked, *why would you ask a dumb question like that?* My response to is—to simply make you think. Think before you spend thousands of dollars on a wonderful wedding planner, perfect wedding invitations—just to impress a group of people who really don't like you and only a handful of relatives that really love you—just for a big show. From the back of the groom and bride head, you stare out into the audience as you dance to your favorite song. You both notice people are drinking and eating and having private, whispered conversations...and it's going to take about three years to pay for this wedding. By the end of the night you both are very exhausted and tired, worn out from all the fake smiles and hugs that you've given to people who really don't love you.

Believe it or not!

You can spend twenty to twenty-five dollars at a local court house and be married for a lifetime—when it's built on truth. This is not reality television. Nobody in the world has the perfect mate. People may pretend its perfect by smiling at each other, fake hugs and kisses—but it's only an Oscar performance. Now, what's real is when a husband and wife get into a big argument: cussing each other out, talking about each other's past mistakes, slamming doors, etc...But by the end of the night—when there is no more huffing and puffing—they both admit how wrong they were, get on their knees and ask forgiveness from God and each other and sleep silently through the night.

Real love, built on truth, will move forward and last a lifetime. The blame game is one of the devil's favorite tools to trick you and cause confusion in your marriage. Uh—oh! Now, let's continue where we left off...

As the car backs out of the driveway, **James** looks at his wife **Karen** with sweet eyes and a warm smile, running his hands through her hair. And he says, "I am so blessed to have you as my wife. There's no one like you in all the world." She smiles back, her voice cracks and she says, "I love you too, **James.**"

Walking into the restaurant, **James** asked the waitress if it was possible to get the table in the corner where they first fell in love. The waitress replied with a warm smile and a jealous heart, envying **James'** wife. The evening continued very well, but **Karen** began to feel very sick after her meal. So she asked her husband, in a weak voice, could they leave. **James**—being such a gentleman—walked around to her side of the table, gave her a soft hug and a kiss on the forehead and said, "Yes, dear."

He paid for dinner, tipped the valet a twenty and drove off slowly. A few minutes later he received a text from **Susan...Susan** the hoe...but he told he told his wife it was his business partner needing to finalize some information to close a deal. Meanwhile, **Karen** looked at the clock on the dashboard and realized it was very late. His response was, "Honey, it'll only take about an hour."

He opened the door for his wife, turned on all the lights, and helped her upstairs. He pulled out her favorite pajamas and assisted her into the night clothes. He then tucked her into bed. James then raced down the steps, beginning to undo the first three buttons on his shirt. He pops a few blue pills and drives off in the Corvette.

A few miles from their home was a nice little house with a friendly woman—a woman who waved when **James** passed by. She'd moved in about six months ago but nobody knew her name. As **James** got closer to the house, he turned off his headlights, pulled over to the side of the road, popped the hood and put on the hazards. In the midst of the night, he walked toward the house. Without knocking or ringing the doorbell, he walked inside. In the shadow of the darkness, the reflection of candlelight, he could see her well dressed in seductive clothes. He slowly walked up behind her, lifting her hair off her neck and kissed her—

Guess what? Now you figure out what happens next.

In the midst of the fog, a man appeared, walking toward the Corvette. This man is **James**. **James** closed the hood, turned off the hazards and drove off. He slowly began to drive home, feeling very, very little guilt, and pulls into the driveway. He goes inside, uses the downstairs guest bathroom to take a shower. As he finishes his shower, he decides to wash a load of clothes—actually getting rid of evidence. He walks upstairs slowly with a warm cup of tea. As he approached the master bedroom, he could hear the sounds of the television. **James** walks into the bedroom and notices his wife is wide awake.

"Hi, dear," he says, "Are you feeling better? Here's a warm cup of tea."

James hands her the tea. He noticed that the pillow had wet spots from the eyes of someone who'd been crying. But he acted like he never saw it.

"Honey, how was your meeting?" **Karen** asked.

"We're thinking about expanding and we have some investors that are interested in our company. Later in the week we will work out the details."

Hmm...Can you read the writing on the wall?

Blinded by love, we try so hard to believe that we have the perfect mate. We search all of our lives to replace the love, the nurturing, the caring and the affections we receive from the time we enter into this world.

Somebody just asked, *"What do you mean?"*

Well, as a baby, we're born and we are given—as a blessing from God—to a wonderful mother and father. Now, for the next thirty-six months (one to thirty-six months) you become the star of the show. You become the attention as you are pushed in your stroller through the mall. You become the conversation piece at your local church. And you take more pictures than a celebrity who walks down the red carpet. And you're held in the arms of so many wonderful people. You receive more kisses than the leading men and women in the movies. Then one day it's all gone. So you search to replace the most genuine love that costs you nothing. That's why it's so important that we take necessary time and necessary priorities, along with proper planning and information when building a lifelong relationship. All of our lives we've been taught to fix lifelong situations with temporary solutions.

Stop!

I mean stop right now, put this book down, go take a look in the mirror, and tell me what you see. A person with a painted on smile and gray streaks of hair because you chased a fantasy that wasn't real. I guess now you're asking yourself what you can do now. Start off first by telling yourself the truth, accepting the truth, and forgiving yourself for all of your past mistakes.

Hit play on the DVD, we're back in the courtroom...

Your lawyer represents you, your spouse's lawyer represents her...and your little boy or girl has to walk up, take a seat, and be asked a question: *Which one of your parents would you like to live with?* Instantly, your heart and spouse's heart begins to feel the pain of a child that's been forced to make a decision—all because you married without love. As the mother stares into the eyes of this helpless child, their strong yet weak voice becomes frozen. The dad begins to weep because of the pain he's caused an innocent child. The judge begins to ask the child,

"Which one of your parents would you like to live with?"

The child is paralyzed by the love they have for both parents. Sometimes in life we become so selfish in fulfilling our own dreams that we forget about the pain we bring to those who *really, really* love us.

Chapter 3

Making Up for the Wrong Reasons

Starring, you leading lady: **Donna**. Co-starring: **Peter**...

"Ladies and gentlemen, fasten your seat belts, put away electrical devices, and remove large items from near your feet. As the stewardess makes her last check down the aisles, we will be taxing down the run way. We hope you enjoy your flight."

"Hello, sir, would you like something to drink?"

"No. I will just rest and take a nap."

"Okay. Thank you."

Oh my god!

The plain is falling out of the sky! What happened! We are all going to die! We are 30,000 feet in the air...so many things I wanted to do! We are falling 100 feet per second. Looks like it was just yesterday when I got my first bike and dad was teaching me how to ride. I remember taking pictures with Mickey Mouse at Disney Land...Oops! I just threw a ball through Mr. Jones' window—surely we are going to die! I had such a wonderful Sweet-16 birthday party; that's where I met the girl of my dreams. Thanks, dad, for lending me the keys to the car for prom...Oh! I forgot to tell you I'm a 17-year-old!

Oh god we are 20,000 feet! We are all going to die! Everyone is screaming, hollering, and jumping around the plane—you know what—I don't care. I'm going to sit down and die gracefully. No more fussing with my wife, no more dealing with my bad kids...that dead end job that it seems I can't ever leave—

Aw! 10,000 feet! My heart is beating fast. The ground is getting bigger! I don't want to die! I don't want to die! Look down! No one seems to care! Everyone is so busy with their everyday life they haven't noticed the plane falling! 2000 feet before we hit the ground! I can't breath! God! Forgive me! For all my sins! Jesus! Can you save me! 100 feet before we hit the ground...50 feet! 40 feet! 30 feet! 20 feet!
BOOM!

I was just dreaming...

Waking up from the dream, **Peter** was sweating, shaking, and crying because he'd caused so much hurt to his family.

Freeze this thought!

If you were only given three to six months to live—all of your success, social friends, homes, cars—wouldn't even matter. The most valuable thing you would have is time and choosing who to share it with.

Payday! It's Friday and I just got paid!

"Honey, why are you so happy?"

"I'm just feeling good! I just got paid. By the way...I'm sorry about last night, I didn't mean to hit you. But you just keep getting bigger. I hate what I see. Thursday was Ladies' Night, I needed to get away from the house...but I didn't have the money because of the bills you made."

"Well, honey, we need to talk about what bills we are going to pay out of your check."

"Right now is not a good time, woman, just leave me alone. Give me a call later and we will talk about it...later."

Midday, during the day, **Donna** called **Peter**, asking him which bills would they be paying. He said, "I'm not paying any bills out of my check, now deal with it! Don't wait up for me, I won't be home till late. I'll stop by the health club, take a shower, and head to the club." Then he hung up in her face.

Instantly, **Donna** feels sorry for herself. She looks in the mirror and she didn't even like what she saw. She said to herself, *I remember when I was 36-24-36...but after having three kids, I'm a size 22... looks like it happened over night. I just can't seem to stop eating.*

Donna began to prepare kids to go to the nursery at the automotive plant where she worked. The devil whispered in her ear, *go to the bathroom, look in medicine cabinet and take fifty pills...and it will all be over.* She slowly turned on the water in the sink, filled her glass, uncapped the bottles and poured a handful of pills.

"Momma! Momma!" her four year old cried out.

The Spirit of the Lord entered into this child. He busted into the bathroom and gave her a big hug and said, "I love you, Momma! And so does Jesus!"

Donna flushed the pills down the toilet, reached down, picked up her 4-year-old son, and began to weep. She pulled herself together, strapped the kids in their car seats and drove off in her van.

Walking inside the gates to work slowly, she went inside and headed to her office.

"Hi, how are you today?" Mr. Lee said. He gave her a big smile and warm hello.

"Just fine," she answered.

Stop lying!

Now here's a woman who's husband beat her last night, she's suicidal, and the man she has three kids with just hung up on her. And her only response is "*just fine*". We become prisoners of our own lies because we put ourselves on pedestals—pedestals that have been created in our fantasy world through soap operas, television shows, and magazines.

Let's continue...

A small voice spoke to **Donna** and told her, don't give up—everything will be alright. She looked around but didn't see anyone. She proceeded to balance her checkbook, paid mortgage, car payment, lights, a few credit cards, and still had $150 to last two weeks.

As the evening continued (she worked from noon to eight in the evening) she picked up the kids, feeling good about her work day. Being Friday, she stopped for take out. She looked at her cell and noticed she hadn't received any calls from the man she loved. She pulled into driveway, took the kids inside, stepped out to get the food and went back inside. After feeding the kids and herself, she fixed a plate for **Peter**. She begins to do laundry. She took some pants from the dryer and noticed that Peter had a phone number with three initials next to it. **Donna** took the paper and put it in a safe place. But a little voice began to torment her about the number. A few moments later, **Donna** calls her sister Montgomery. Later on, Montgomery shows up at the door.

Ding Dong! Ding Dong!

"What's wrong, Sis? You rarely ever call me anymore."

"Well, I just work, take care of the kids, and try to be a good wife...Hey, I need a big favor. The kids are asleep and I need to run an errand."

"Okay, fine."

"I won't be long."

Donna called a long time friend who is a dispatcher at the local police station.

"I know it's been a long time, Jack, but I need a big favor," **Donna** said.

"Yeah, it's been a long time."

"You know we were just kids back then...my high school sweet heart...Okay here it is. I found this number and I need an address and name."

"You know I can't do that...but because of our history, I'll help you...hold on."

Jack came back to the line. Before he could complete the first and last name, **Donna's** heart dropped. He continued to give her the address. She thanked him and hung up.

Once again the devil told her to drive by the address. As she began to get closer to the house number, she dimmed the lights. Her heart began to race. As big as day, there was **Peter's** SUV. Donna drove off fast, tears running down her face...hitting the steering wheel and banging on the dashboard. Unfocused, she ran the red light. It seemed like the longest ride she'd taken home.

Donna unlocked the door, went inside, and dropped to her knees. Her sister ran to her and asked,

"What's wrong! What's wrong!"

"I have given this dirty, low down, dog fifteen years of my life. Put him through school, had his three kids, keep our home clean...washing his dirty underwear..."

"I tell you what, lets call our sister Kim," Montgomery suggested..."Hello, Kim?"

"Who is this?"

"Girl, this is your sister. We need you right away. Stop whatever you are doing and get over here! **Donna** has issues!"

The next thing you hear are breaks squeaking in the driveway.

"Girl," Montgomery started, "I told you from the first time I met him that I knew something wasn't right. He was winking at me! Momma tried to tell you. Daddy tried to tell you. And I tried to tell you not to marry the man! Okay...what do you need me to do? **Donna**, lets take a ride...pull yourself together... we got your back...Girl, stop at this gas station and let me fill up this gas can..."

"Okay..."

"**Donna**, pull over around the corner. Turn the lights off and you stay right here. I'll be right back."

Montgomery began to walk towards the SUV. She pulls her hood up, checks around to make sure no one is watching...runs over to the SUV, drenches it with gasoline and set the truck on fire. She ran back to **Donna's** van and they sped off fast.

"Girl, I don't believe what you just did!"

"Look, **Donna**, you better not tell anybody. You promise?"

A few minutes later, **Donna** calls Kim from the cell phone.

"We're on our way back. Girl, your sister is crazy.

Donna unlocks the door and they all sit down for some coffee.

"Girl! What happened? Y'all seem so happy," Kim said.

"I don't know...I thought we *were* happy," **Donna** shrugged.

"Who is this hoe, you let steal your man!" Montgomery demanded.

THE DEVIL IS A LIAR!

When we face the truth about the life we work so hard to build and it seems like all it's all a lie from day-one—what do we do? Call your lawyer—nah, I'm just playing! Get on your knees, and ask God to give you guidance.

Here are five quotes:

- "Just kill him!"—wrong answer. You thought wrong. Your understanding of what makes a man happy is wrong. By having sex with him does not mean you love him. Were your motives pure or devilish? You are a woman of high caliber, but you live in a world that never existed.
- Before we are married we normally receive three to five calls a day from our mate. We go on dates and cost is not a factor and time is a beautiful luxury.
- I have seen the signs but love continuously blinds those signs. Sometimes in life, we put ourselves on a pedestal. We have the perfect body, very attractive, good paying job, nice car and no one to share it all with. Then we say to ourselves, *"What person wouldn't have me?"*
- Being the star of attention we seem to put ourselves on pedestals; building on false words of encouragement.
- Life is not fair. It takes work, a true relationship with Jesus Christ, and a whole lot of prayer.

Donna asked her sisters to give her a few minutes alone and asked if they could watch the kids for a moment. She begins to drive in circles saying to herself, *Lord, why have you deserted me? Help me understand why I must suffer so much for* *a man I love. Whom I have given my best to. Help me please! Give me guidance on what to do with my life at this tragic time. I'm lost. I'm tired. And, I'm confused. I can't understand. We work together. We had lunch sometimes. We went shopping after work occasionally...*

It seemed like all night she'd been driving but it had only been a half an hour...

Tears begin to fall down **Donna's** face. Her shirt started getting wet. A few seconds later, she received a text from her sisters asking when she would be home. **Donna** apologized and a few minutes later she drove home into the driveway. As she entered the front door, she begins to tell her sisters...

"I knew for a long time things weren't right. He stopped taking me out after the first baby. Fewer calls just to say hello...only time he had for me was bedtime. He stopped noticing and telling me how attractive I am...And that hoe laughed in my face, asking me questions about my kids and my family. And all the time she was having a relationship with my husband! And that dirty, low down dog—I'm gonna get him someday. He crushed my heart! I have never ever hated like this before."

Three in the morning and **Donna** is waiting for **Peter** to come home. She can hear a car creeping toward the house, the car door slamming, then the car drove off fast. She could hear the keys rattling. As the door unlocked, she could hear the sound of every foot step. She noticed he stopped by the kids' rooms, walked into the master bedroom—and didn't speak to her. **Peter** went to the master bathroom, took a hot shower, and got into bed. He rolled over to his side and went to sleep.

Donna began to cry, saying to herself, *He acts like nothing ever happened.*

Being Saturday morning, the kids go up early and ran into the room to give their mom and dad big kisses.

Peter said, "I love you."

Donna got out of bed and cleaned up the kids. **Peter** went downstairs to cook breakfast. When **Donna** and the kids came downstairs, they could smell and hear the sound of bacon frying. **Peter's** back was towards the oven. **Donna** picked up a knife, looking at him while he was cooking. The devil told her, *Stab him! In his back! Do it! I say do it!* But the love **Donna** had for him was so strong, she began to cry.

"What are you doing?" **Peter** turned around and asked.

Donna dropped the knife, ran up to their master bedroom and closed the door. **Peter** ran after her shouting,

"Are you crazy! I said are you!"

"No! You dirty dog! I hate you!"

He turned around and began to head back downstairs. He asked for the keys to her van.

"Walk!" **Donna** shouted.

And then, with a very nervous and scared voice, she asked, "What does she have that I don't have? Tell me. I'll work on it. Please give me that chance. Would you like me to try new things with you?"

Silence...

"Nine, one, one, what's your emergency?"
"I just shot my husband!"
"Ma'am, calm down. Repeat yourself!"
"I said, I just shot my husband!"
"Ma'am, is he breathing?"
"I don't know! But blood is everywhere!"
"Ma'am, who's that voice?"
"My kids crying...Stop crying babies!"

"Hello, Mom? I shot him!"
"Oh, my god! What have you done! Where are the kids?"
Mom was so disturbed that she dropped the phone. You could hear Dad in the background asking what happened. Dad snatches up the phone.
"What happened?"
"Dad, don't let them take my kids!"
"What are you talking about?"
"Police are everywhere!" **Donna** cried.
"Okay, dear, we are on our way!"

Few moments later...

"Sir, let me inside. It's my daughter and my grandchildren. I'm her father and this is her mother."
"Sir, stand behind the yellow line! This is a homicide scene!"
"Who do we need to talk to? We just want to see her and the kids!"

"Reporting live from channel seven! This is Yvonne Carline. There seems to be gunshots fired this morning in this very prosperous and upstanding neighborhood! Beside me is Melvin. Melvin called nine-one- one shortly after hearing several gunshots."

"I ran over to the neighbor's house, looked through the window and saw **Donna** *holding the gun! She was crying, the baby was crying, and she was trying to console the other two kids. Blood was everywhere! Few seconds later police were surrounding the house. I just don't understand why she did it. A wonderful couple and beautiful children...they both have great jobs, a big house, nice cars, and a lot of friends always over..."*

Melvin began to cry and the reporter stopped filming to comfort him.

"All I have been hearing is wonderful things about this perfect couple and their beautiful children...Roll the cameras! They are bringing her out of the house!"

She's in handcuffs...both grandparents accommodating the children...Dad being such a proud man, decided to put a towel over **Donna's** head. The entire neighborhood became still and silent. As the police car drove off slowly, everyone gathered in small groups and began to whisper about what they thought happened...

Your life just changed!

How long will you stay in a relationship that could permanently damage and affect so many lives? And all based on one bad decision. Now, in this scenario, one life is taken and another will have to rot in jail while demons torment her. If only you had taken time to build this relationship on truth, purpose, and fulfilling each other's happiness in life—not just at bed time. But look at the bright side—this is not you!

Let's continue...

"Order in the court!"

The judge whispers in a strong voice, "Has the jury reached a verdict?"

The little old lady stood up and said," Yes, Your Honor. We find the defendant guilty of all charges."

Donna's mother began to cry and her dad stared at the jury with eyes of a murderer. If he had the chance, he would kill them all.

The oldest child, being held and comforted by grandma, had no idea what was going on. **Donna's** side of the family was in tears. **Peter's** side was filled with joy and sadness.

"Lock down! It's ten fifteen. Lights out! Good night ladies!" The guard announced.

You only have a small light and you're writing your children to tell them how you love and miss them. You spend most of your life serving time and writing people who will never understand. You learn to appreciate little things in life and big things suddenly become meaningless. Saying, "Good night, roommate" *to a stranger who is just like you as you both fall asleep...*

"Mama! Mama! Mama!"

Subconsciously **Donna** hears this voice in her sleep. She woke up, realizing it was all a dream. She began to scream at the top of her lungs. She hugs and kisses her kids. **Peter** bursts into the room.

"What is wrong with you, crazy woman!"

"I'm free! I'm free! Thank you, Jesus, I'm free!"

"What do you mean?"

"I want a divorce. I'm going to lose all this weight. Check me out in a few months! See ya and get out!"

Chapter 4

Giving Sex to get Love

1963

The high school football team is going to the championship game. Kathy, head cheerleader, was invited to a party hosted by the quarterback. Everybody who was somebody in the school was invited.

As Kathy drove up near the house, she could hear loud music. The girls and guys were dressed cool and everyone was having fun. And you know Kathy could not make her debut without a flash. She was loved by the boys and hated by the girls.

Kathy slowly walked in her short Versace miniskirt and Dunny and Burk handbag. She went inside looking for Jay, the quarterback. Jay was being entertained by half of the cheerleading squad and receiving hugs and kisses from the other half. Kathy instantly became jealous. Fits of rage began to run through her body. So she did what any 17-year-old high school cheerleader would do—she asked the running back, Joe, to dance. She became very seductive and aggressive; succeeding in making Jay jealous before the song was finished.

Kathy looked across the room and saw Jay whispering for her. He began to talk to her for a moment and asked if she wanted to see the rest of the house. Jay's family had the biggest house in the neighborhood. His dad was a banker and his mom was a lawyer.

So after showing her all the beautiful rooms, Jay interested her in showing his room. By this time, she knew he had to have her. Being the school hoe, Kathy was just playing her role: she had sex with boys just to get attention.

1964: Prom Night

Its prom night and the theme is "Aloha! Hawaiian Prom." Kathy didn't even have a date because she'd been with half the football team. Everybody talked about her. Desperate times call for desperate measures, so she asked her best friend's brother to the prom. He was on vacation from college for the weekend.

As he pulled up in the driveway, approached the house, a stunning young woman answered the door. He said hello to the family and they were off. Half way through the night of prom, Kathy became sloppy drunk, dancing wildly and seductively—being her normal self. By the end of prom, her date asked her for a kiss. Before the clock stroke midnight, she'd had sex on school grounds. He drove her home, dropped her at the door and never said good night.

Early Saturday morning, Kathy woke up with a bad headache. She looked bad, smelled worse, and the prom dress was filthy. Her mom asked,

"How was the dance, honey?"

"It was the greatest prom ever!"

Monday morning everybody is back in school. It was only a few days left until graduation. Everybody was laughing at Kathy. They were talking, pointing, and making faces at her. She became so emotionally disturbed that she left school early. She advised her parents they would have to have her diploma mailed to her. Her mom had no understanding why. Kathy's only reply,

"Get over it, Mom. It's not going to happen."

1981

Kathy is driving down the highway singing, "*Summer time! Summer time!*"

She was listening to her favorite talk show host and she decided to call in today.

"Go 'head, caller! You are listening to GGTG Hot Praise with your girl, Lady Praise. Listener, what is your question?"

"I just can't keep a man," Kathy said.

"Girl, tell me why you think you just can't keep a man."

"Well, we go on a few dates and before you know, we have sex and it's all over."

"Well, the problem seems you should start by keeping your clothes on. Second, you don't have a good choice of men! Third, how are you dressing on these dates! Are you dressing to have sex or are you dressing to have a long term relationship?"

Kathy became very quiet.

"Caller, you still there?" Lady Praise asked.

"Yes..." she answered in a whisper.

"Well, girlfriend let me give you some sister advice. Start feeling good about yourself. Start dressing nice and stop talking so much. Next time you go on a date, ask for these three things. One, a paycheck stub. Two, last year's tax return. And three, a receipt showing the down payment for your ring. And no sex!"

"You are so right!"

"Listen, you can't afford to keep rolling the dice with your life. You may end up with AIDS or some type of STD. Now your life is over before it even started. You want all life has promised to you. You do not want to wake up one morning and be sixty, still living alone. I believe every woman will be given an opportunity to meet the man that God has created for her. With a little prayer and a little faith you will meet him. Do we fight our mom for not teaching us or fight ourselves for making bad choices? Girl, I love you. I'm gonna send this song out for you.

Alright, be blessed. Let us pay some bills and we'll be right back.

"Go 'head, caller, you're live with Lady Praise. Girlfriend, what's your question?"

"Yes, do you think a hot body will keep a man?"

"Girlfriend, if all you have is your body to keep your man, you won't keep him long. So many people believe that sex is the answer to true love and happiness!"

But the devil is a liar!

"You put yourself on this pampered pedestal, created by love novels, television shows, and commercials. But let me give my sisters all over the world some good advice. Dress for success... to one day make a good wife to a good man. But with today's fashion and hip sayings, we dress for an audition as a playboy centerfold. In reality, those women are very insecure, with low self esteem, and have slept with every man from the mail man to the pool pit. Let's uncover the core problem deep inside a broken hearted woman. Hurt, pain, betrayal, usury, deception and manipulation are all seeds that keep us in bondage like this. Listener, stop crying, pull over to the side of the road and get yourself together."

Even the persons reading this book—

"Every man is not a dog. Every man is not a liar. Pray and ask Jesus to help you next time you go on a date. I will send this song out to you. And to all the fellas that may be listening to this live show, you will find the wife that was created for you. And we are back live with you girl Lady Praise. Can I just keep it real for a minute? Ladies, you are created to be a great wife to a great man. Sometimes in life, relationships derail because of impure motives and the insecurities of not being able to compete with the girl next door. Take for example, myself. I had a purpose in life—to make my husband a very proud man. To nurture and groom my children, to be humble and be everyday people. Now don't get it wrong, I'm not a perfect host, but I have also been created to serve others. And by serving others I become a servant of God. Expecting nothing for myself, leaving room to grow—Oh! The lines are lighting up! Go 'head caller! What's your name?"

"Mark."

"What's your question, Mark?"

"I keep dating women who just want to spend my money and have sex. That is getting old and I am not getting younger. So now my life seems different for whatever reason. And second part to my question, how do I choose a good woman?"

"What a very good question, Mark. Mark, oh my god the lines just lit up! Mark, tell me how would you like your new wife to be?"

"Well, she' doesn't have to be the most beautiful woman in the world to others. As long as she's beautiful to me. I don't want a gold-digger. I want her to be trustworthy and reliable. And I would like her to be able to have three children, but there is room to negotiate. I don't want her to tear me down when I make mistakes and use words to discredit my manhood. I'm not looking for a momma and I definitely am not looking for a daddy—I'm already grown. But I prefer a lady that will mold me and shape me into the prince of her life. And allow me to shape her into the princess of my life. Now if she's listening to this broadcast, I promise to never cheat on her, always spend time with her, call her during the day, and never let any other woman disrespect her. I promise to call her when I'm running late, and get along with my mother-in-law."

"Caller, hold on! We have to pay some bills!"

Ladies, don't judge!

Most women have so much baggage from past life that when their real man shows up—they don't have the ability to adapt or accept what is good. You have eaten the forbidden fruit of evil and when good fruit is presented, you can't deal with it.

"Hello, caller?"

"I'm still here, Praise. I'm still here."

"I hear so much anger and hurt in your voice, Mark."

"Yes, because I hate her and I hate her today."

"Who are you talking about?" Praise asked.

"The woman that cut my heart out over thirteen years ago. Her name was Kathy. I went from being a good man to being voted player club of the year. The girls were named Monday, Tuesday, Wednesday,

Thursday, Friday, Saturday, and Sunday. I learned after that, you give gifts, you get sex. I have never been the same since that day..."

"Hello, caller, you okay?"

"That hoe broke my heart and it still hurts today."

"Caller, come back!...Oops, audience, the call dropped. If he calls back, put him right through. But we are going to pray this prayer for you, Mark. Father, in heaven, heal his broken heart. Fix his mind to trust you with his life. Teach him how to forgive from then until now. In Jesus name, Amen."

Why?

Sometimes sex is used to show love. In a way, you hide your true feelings. We have no other way, if we are not taught, to show love without being physical.

"You are live at GGTG Hot Praise with Lady Praise! Go 'head caller."

"My name is Susan. My question is, why do men roll over after having sex, get on their side of the bed, and go straight to sleep?"

"Good question, Susan. Let's play back what happened before bedtime. It took so much time to get you there, Susan, that after the man finished there was a breakdown in communication. Have you ever taken time to teach your man how to be sensitive at a time like this? That's your job if you are a real woman. If you want your man to be sensitive and accommodate your needs, you must develop him, motivate and encourage him. Now, remember, you had fun too. Try this next time you're together at bedtime—you roll over and hug him and this will show him action. Do not belittle him with bad words. Be blessed. This is yo girl, Lady Praise. Go 'head caller."

"It's your boy and his name is One-time."

"What's your questions, One-time?"

"Well, my wife is getting older but not me. We have been married twenty-five years. She's still beautiful with a beautiful body. But at bed time she dresses like a seventy-five-year-old, retired, grandmother. Back in my hay days she would dress like a Playboy centerfold. What can I do to help her, Lady Praise?"

"Very, very, very good question. Often when women become married, over time they just forget because other things become priority. They just stop taking care of themselves. Now, ladies, I stopped by to set the record straight about that old cliché 'whatever it took to get him, it's gonna take all that and some to keep him.' Girlfriend, don't get it twisted! Don't think just because you got a couple of kids, beautiful house, a big diamond on your finger, Mercedes parked in the driveway—that an 18-year-old secretary wont steal your man! Okay most women don't think that staying married is important sometimes. You must learn to distinguish the purpose you were created for. We devalue ourselves and miss great opportunities by playing games with the devil. Your bad girl syndrome will cause you to lose everything and one day you will be sitting in that rocking chair all alone...Go 'head caller, what's your question?"

"My husband only has time for me at bedtime. How do I fix this problem?"

"Good question. Two answers. One, if you build your relationship on looks, what you wear, and your body, then your husband will only see you has a sex machine and not a wife. He would rather watch football on Sunday than communicate with you on unimportant things. Both of you have been taught wrong. The people who have influenced you—mom, dad, co-workers—probably had some problems of their own. It is impossible to fix a problem if you have been taught wrong. Second answer to your question, you built your marriage without a relationship with God. Most people in the world become each other's gods. For example, we lie to each other, we have sex before marriage, we have impure motives, we manipulate because we are used to getting what we want. Then there are our selfish desires...fairy tale relationships...and after a few dates you engage in a sexual relationship that is built on lust of the eye, unrated commercials, etc. But it is not love! After all is said and done, you get marred. And when your honeymoon is over, your major conversation is 'when are we going to pay these bills?'"

"Well, that's great and that is all true. How do we fix the problem?"

"Very good response. Start by telling each other the truth, confess your sins to each other, and take one day at a time. Pray for deliverance in the relationship. Pray not to be used under demonic sexual influence. Pray for open communication and set one day apart to have fun together. And never give up. Amen. Well, let's pay some bills..."

"Go 'head, caller. What is your question?"

"I cheated on my wife and I can't deal with it anymore. What do I do?"

"Caller, keep on keeping it real. I like the way you started of by telling the truth. My advice to you is to ask God for forgiveness. Tell your wife the truth, ask her for forgiveness, and then trust God to work it out for both your lives. Thank you for being honest. Most people would take that to their grave. But there is no secret under the sun that God doesn't know. This has been the greatest show I have ever hosted in my life. Next caller."

"I don't believe my child is my husband's. I had a one-night stand with my ex from back in the day. I was mad at my husband because he didn't buy me that new car...and he cheated on me with his ex when we first got married. I though I had forgiven him, but I hadn't. That made it easy for me to sleep with my ex. As my son begins to get older, I notice he is starting to look different from my other children. My husband really loved him when he was a baby and spent many hours just putting him to sleep. I knew in my heart something wasn't right. Lately, my husband has distanced himself from our son. I need to tell him the truth, but I am afraid I will lose everything. My husband will leave me and go on with his life. He's a very, very, proud man. He would rather pay child support and alimony than stay with me. My biggest nightmare is if our son was to get sick and we found out this wasn't his son. That would be a major problem. Praise, I am so afraid."

"Girl, you have a problem that only God can fix for you. Telling him the truth will only set you free. In reality you have become a very proud woman and it keeps you from telling the truth. You and I both know your husband would leave you. But that is not the problem. The real problem is you scaling down to a smaller house, leaving behind the social life you have developed, taking the kids from private to public school...what you talk about with local soccer moms and the prayer warriors you used to read and pray with. Hm-hm-hm! I can't help you. Call your local pastor because you are about to lose everything. Girl, pray for God to intervene on your behalf. Pray he steps in! Callers, I can feel her hurt and pain. Go 'head caller, what's your question?"

"I lied to get married. I told him I was pregnant, but it was a hoax. A few weeks after our honeymoon, I told him I lost the baby. Now, I can't even get pregnant. Do you think God cursed me because I lied? He's a good man, but I don't love him. He bought me a big house, we drive nice cars, and girl, if you could see the ring on my finger...seven karats...Help me, Praise."

"What kind of woman would have to lie to get a man to marry her? You don't deserve to be recognized as a wife...or a woman at this point in your life. You have made me angry. It is women like you who were created before time to be a help mate and help your man. Now, you have created a situation that if God doesn't heal that man completely, he is going create havoc in many women's lives. A real woman would have never put herself in that position. You premeditated a plot to trick a man that could have been the best husband to come in your life. Repent, ask God to forgive you, tell him the truth and pray God's mercy on you. You better hope God can fix this. Otherwise, you will lose that good man. I tell you the truth, sex can not fix everything. I gotta take a commercial break."

"Callers, callers...Go 'head, what is your question?"

"I don't love my wife. I love my ex. Every time we are intimate, I think about my ex. I use my wife's body but I close my eyes and see my ex. What do you think, Praise? She keeps trying everything she can to make me happy. She's the perfect little wife. Anything I need, she gives it to me without thinking twice. Bed time, she dresses pretty for me, she keeps the house immaculate...Every evening I come home, and I can smell and have a hot dinner. She gives me her paychecks every two weeks to pay the bills. She is every man's dream wife. But I do not love her. My heart belongs to my ex. I need help, Lady Praise. I was blind to my selfish desires. Her family had plenty of money...on our honeymoon night, I thought about my ex. Now, it hurts to keep using her like this. I cheat on her in my mind with my ex everyday."

"Boy, I tell you, you got a mess on your hands. I tell you—is anybody married for real?! All the thousands of dollars wasted on the wedding and honeymoon...Her mother and father will be devastated—not because of the money, but to see their daughter's life destroyed. You should have told her the truth before you said I do. You would rather have hurt her then, than to destroy her life now. You can't have your ice cream and cake too. It is totally against God's will of 'they shall become one flesh'...Hello? Hello? Caller? Oops, the call dropped. Go 'head caller, what's your question?"

"The love for my kids keeps me in an abusive relationship. It breaks my heart and destroys my mind every time he beats me up then makes me have sex with him. It feels like he's raping me over and over. Help me, Lady Praise."

"Ma'am, my heart dropped to the floor just to hear you tell such an awesome story. Right about now, I feel like getting in my car, driving over with a baseball bat and hitting him in his head. But God would get no glory out of that. Do you have family you and your kids can stay with until you get a job? I know you feel like you're in a prison when you have to depend on his money to support you and the kids."

"Things changed after I stopped working and had our third child. We stay locked up in this house all day. I can't visit my parents, my family, former co-workers...Don't get me wrong, he takes very good care of me and the kids. We live in a very upstanding neighborhood, we attend our local church...Love can blind you sometimes. He grabbed me a few times and shook me while we were dating. But I was too blind to see that as a sign. And I only found out he was a control freak after we got married. I had to call every time me and the kids left home. One Christmas we went to my parents' house. The kids were having a fun. My brothers and sisters were there with my nieces and nephews...and for just a moment, I felt free. After two hours, he was ready to go. He has beaten all of the love out of my heart—Oh! Oh! He's pulling up in the driveway! I gotta go—I gotta go!"

Busy signal...

Tears began to fall from Lady Praise's eyes. But, she prays this prayer:

"Master, I pray for my sister, where she's calling from, heal her husband. Fix his mind. Open a door for her and her children to be safe. Audience, after hearing a call like this, I must sign off and send this song out to you. It's been good talking to you all. See you, tomorrow. Keep it real."

A few moments later, two cars pull up to the red light. Both cars have the same radio station blasting loud. Kathy pulls up in her red convertible Corvette and Mark in his BMW. They look over at each other with big smiles and drive off slowly...the rest is history...

To be continued...

The writer of this book has challenged you to find the hidden ending to this chapter in this book, featuring Kathy and Mark...

Chapter 5

Somebody Plays the Fool

Before you leave this world, you will be somebody's fool. Whether it is past, present, or future—you will play the fool. Ironically, most people don't realize they are somebody's fool until it is too late. You try to suppress the truth with a lie based on your ego; an ego that has been created by your selfishness, your arrogance, your impure motives and believing that little voice that whispers in your ear. Because of your street smarts, years given to gracefully obtain wisdom and education-you really believe your game is tight. Every game that people play will break down because it was built with a lie.

There are two types of game players. There is the one that actually sits down and premeditates a plan to make somebody their fool. Let me give you a clear definition because somebody is going to challenge this. For example: using your body in exchange for someone paying your house payment, car payment, overextended credit cards, a shopping spree on Rodale Drive...

Now, the second kind of game player has been scared, manipulated, and falsely influenced, and totally tricked. This person's reward is total revenge. They are hurt by backlashes of someone's ego, the hell and evil that other people have caused them. The side effects of those actions have created ticking time bombs of bitterness, low self-esteem, and living in this world alone.

The secrets people will hide...

Black Diary

Volume 1: written by Lauren

Dear Diary,

I just came off a date with this egotistical, selfish man who thinks he is God's gift to women—and all because of his nice physic, being the executive of a fortune 500 company, and his boy toy cars. This is a fool for the taking. I am going to use him up, break down his confidence, and dwindle his bank account. He will suffer for all the men that have used my body, sent my mind on a roller coaster twister, and broken promise after promise...lied to me and I never made it to the alter...

I made this fool spend three hundred dollars on our first dinner date. I pushed the limit. I ordered food that cost the most on the menu. As we slowly dove near my house, he pretended to be a gentleman and opened my door and escorted me to my front door. I enticed him to come closer. His weak, pathetic mind thought I was going to give him a kiss and then invite him inside. But, I said goodnight. Fifteen minutes later, when I thought he was almost home, I called just to play games with his mind. I told him I was so blessed to meet him and I could not wait to see him again. And using my seductive voice, I whispered, I wish you were here right now, just to hug me and hold me tight. *His response was,* Baby, I could turn around and be there in twenty minutes. *With a girly voice, I said,* Maybe next time. *I just planted a seed in his foolish mind. He is going to suffer for all the men that used me. I have no intentions of ever having sex with that man. He is a joke and don't even know it, with those 70s and 80s played out lines at dinner. It's just like taking candy from a baby. Smiling and inter-acting is just part of the plan for the next two months. I am about to experience Christmas everyday with this fool. I'm going to slowly walk him to the cliff, build the excitement, leading him on, and push him off the cliff.*

Most men don't know we are aware that after they spend all that money, they are looking for something in return. Well, he just met his match. Good night, Diary.

Good afternoon, Diary,

That fool has called me three times and left messages. I have no intentions of calling back today.

I have to make this hunt an exciting one for him. I am not easy prey. At this time, I have to see just how bad he wants me. Ha! And my girls enjoyed the leftovers from the dinner that fool paid for last night. We laughed and made fun of his played out lines. Alright, Diary, I have to get back to work. I'll check in later.

Good morning, Diary,

I left a message this morning on his cell phone telling him I woke up with him on my mind and I could not wait to see him. I will take his call today. There is a big concert in town this week and I heard the tickets were around two hundred dollars. I am going to plant a seed by telling him that my girl-friends and their dates are going to the concert. Then I am going to let him talk about it, by telling him I'm going to spend time home all alone...maybe take mom to the grocery store, come home and watch television. Guarantee, he is going to say, How about I get us some tickets to the concert. *Then I will say,* I am going out to buy some nice outfits and we can go window shopping. *Then I will let him buy my shoes and accessories...rub my breasts against his chest and kiss him on the cheek. Diary, I am so bad...*

The End

Black Diary

Volume 2: written by Dr. Lorraine

It would break my husband's heart if he knew that I had a relationship with one of the nurses. The secret relationship has been going on for two years and I have to lock you up at work. If anyone were to find and read this, Diary, it would destroy my life. But I have to tell someone and the only one I trust is you, Diary.

Last summer, while we were on vacation, I called my lover twenty-one times and they called me on my secret cell phone forty-one times. I was in the shower, after being intimate with my husband, crying over leaving my lover. I felt I had betrayed them. So, I got my secret cell phone and took nude pictures and sent it to them. Using this as a tool to energize their oppressed mind...

On my way to dinner, my husband told me how proud he was of me and all my accomplishments, giving me a big kiss and a wonderful hug. The problem, Diary, is that I love my husband, he is a good man. But I have feelings so strong toward my lover that I can't let go. I feel ashamed and dirty after being with my lover, ever time my husband tells me he loves me. Hm!

Last year, I had to give away all the gifts my lover gave me to friends and family. Suddenly, I had the urge to ask my husband to take me out to the restaurant where I knew my lover would be. I wanted to be able to see them and flirt with them every time my husband took his eyes off me. I specially asked for the table across from where my lover was sitting. My husband never knew all of my coworkers, so...I noticed my lover slowly walking toward the bathroom...I gracefully excused myself from the table at the same time...in the dark shadows, the rest hidden, I walked slow enough to intentionally bump into my lover. We made eye contact, my heart began to accelerate and then I intentionally bumped into them with my breasts. Ooh! It felt so good.

We continued dinner, my love and I ordered the same dish. My husband tipped the valet. While he was distracted, I turned around and blew my lover a kiss... Driving home and listening to my favorite CD that my lover bought for me, talking to my husband, engaging in nice conversation.

I dressed seductively with the lingerie that my lover bought for me; closed my eyes tight to be intimate with my husband...but I only see my lover...I almost called the name of my lover—oh! You bad girl, from the dark side! Good night, Diary.

Good morning, Diary,

My husband is asleep and I had to talk to you. My life is so off track, I need to break it off with my lover but I don't know how. My heart is divided in two parts. My husband has one half and m lover has the other. I'm going to hell for cheating on my husband. This is not a game. People's lives can be destroyed. People's families can be altered and destinies can be changed. The way my luck goes I may end up losing both of them. Well, Diary, I gotta get dressed for work. See ya later.

Hi, Diary,

My day has been full of "I love you" kisses to my lover. I kissed my lover five times in our secret closet. It is lunch time and I guess I'll sit in the cafeteria so I can see my lover.

"Paging Doctor Lorraine! Paging Doctor Lorraine! Paging Doctor Lorraine! Code red!"

She panicked, jumped up from her desk, leaving her diary. She didn't know her wonderful husband had packed a picnic basket filled with her favorite foods. He also bought a dozen white roses—symbolizing their purity and trust in their relationship—showing up a few minutes after she got the page. He made rare appearances to the hospital because of his wife's busy schedule. But this was their 10-year anniversary. He tried to surprise her when he could.

Entering into the hospital with beautiful flowers and purple basket drew a lot of attention. As he approached the receptionist desk, Lorraine's lover advised him they had a code red emergency. Her lover then offered to escort him to Lorraine's office; he could lounge there until she came back. He placed the picnic basket and flowers on her desk and stared at the pictures of past vacations…he noticed this little black diary, so he picked it up and, like any man would do, began to read.

Black Diary

Volume 3: written by Susan

The world is coming to an end. I slept with a television evangelist, a preacher of the cloth and gospel. He gave me $2000 but I think he didn't know I knew who he was. People fail to realize that sometimes at our lowest points in life, even a sinner will watch Christian television.

He over talked himself, talking about things that have no value to me...something about how he fantasizes about having sex, unrated sex, with a professional. I worked my magic and he will be back at $2000 a pop. The bottom line, it is not even worth that, but ego-driven men with big attitudes and weak silly wives make my job easier everyday. It is the difference between selling a Volkswagen and a Mercedes. You just dress it up.

The downside of being in this position, I've watched men splurge and spend their kids' college funds just to have a good time with me. And the only one who loses is those helpless, innocent children. I have caused Forbes Fortune 500 CEOs to leave their multimillion dollar homes at midnight so I could work my magic. Remember this—a rich dog and a poor dog have the same needs. But a dog is just another dog.

Just last month, this real estate agent had a commission check for $3000, I knew. His mortgage payment was due, he and his wife's car payment was due. He needed lunch money for the kid and daycare *expenses...but a good time with me caused him to get kicked out of his house. Just last night I had a principal of a high school beat his wife so he could come and see me naked. Another quick $2000 from a weak, silly little boy trying to play in a man's world.*

Going to the Mercedes dealership, I knew my credit score wasn't strong, so I walked in there half naked. I wore my Rolex watch, $1500 pair of Stilettos— dressed to take candy from a baby. I asked to test drive my Mercedes advising the salesman I needed to speak to the owner—and the owner only. I pulled out his business card that he had given me last year after paying me $2000 and advised him of what I wanted. He got up from his desk and went over to the original salesman who helped me and told him he would be taking over the deal.

It has always been easy for me, Diary. I remember when I couldn't pay my gas bill. The gas service worker came to turn my gas off. I advised him I wasn't able to make arrangements to pay and invited him in for a cool glass of lemonade. I never paid a gas bill after that. Just by lying on my back... I must be the daughter of the Devil. I have slept with over 1000 men since I was thirteen. I could never marry my prince charming because I am so dirty.

Now I have learned to hate myself. My body is just a money maker. I have become a rich hoe on fulfilling the desires, weaknesses, and fantasies of men. I have had the privilege of dating governors of big states. I recall this one incident that the body guard of a governor threatened to kill me and my family or anyone I ever told. So this one I will take to my grave. Federal employees...mail carriers, have delayed mail just to come see me. Money has the authority to make one powerful and prosperous. It is my job to break the bank of every weak, silly man. When you sell your soul to the Devil, you have to pay him back with interest. He gives you the power to do evil things and he gives you demonic influences with sexual desires... To destroy the lives of every man I have ever slept with. It is a crying shame when a man sleeps around and he never thinks about the damage he costs his family.

I have no conscience. I send those little boys back home without enough money to pay just one little bill. I have been given great opportunities. I attended a banquet of a former president. If I had only had five minutes alone with this man, just to drop to my knees...Women-like myself- who use the power of sex to control their husbands, boyfriends, fiancés, make me very rich. Every time they say no, I say yes.

The owners of Fortune 500 companies pay me $1000 a week. One is the owner of a lot of property and I have not paid rent in seven years...what a fool. His poor wife is a joke to me. She drives around in her nice car and with her fancy friends...the only reason he has not left her is because he doesn't want to give her half. Oops, time to go, Diary. Talk to you later.

I'm back! Just made $2000 with this lawyer who lives in this upscale community. His kids go to a very outstanding private school. His wife works as a community volunteer, giving all her time but she *doesn't have time for her own husband. He calls me about three times a month just to spend thousands. Just last week I gave a judge a free one—I needed a DWI fixed and kept off my file. But what he didn't know is that every occasion I spend time with him, I recorded it all. Being in high places with powerful people, I have heard a lot of powerful things. I have hung out with big name bands, leaving their Barbie doll-fake wives at the hotel. I have slept with Grammy Award winners and multi-platnum selling artists—ooh I have been feeling sick lately. I will call my doctor, who is on call twenty four seven and leave a message for a call back.*

He called me back and I began to describe my illness to him. He advised me he needed to run some tests right away.

"Hello, Doc? Hello? Doc, you there?"
My cell phone dropped...

_____

_____

_____

_____

_____

_____

_____

_____

_____

_____

The dark side of a woman...

In the beginning of time, Eve was manipulated by Satan. He began to have a very focused conversation with her. But God still allowed it. If you have found yourself in any of these characters, it is important to repent, ask God to forgive you for all of the families you have destroyed, and accept Jesus Christ into your heart. He is willing to forgive you and give you the opportunity to start a band new life right now. Amen.

Black Diary

Volume 4: written by Stacy

Dear Diary,

I pray nobody in my lifetime reads this diary...not until I am dead. That evil witch, so-called momma, I hate her with a passion. I could never forgive her. I am overwhelmed and over burdened that I have to release this. One night, at the age of seven, my step-father came into my room...he began to talk to me and tell me things I had no understanding of at the time. He began to touch me inappropriately on parts of my body. He took my hand and placed it on inappropriate parts of his body. Clear as day, I began to cry. He placed his hands over my mouth, looked me in my eyes with the eyes of a killer. He told me he would kill my mother if I ever told anyone. It continued for weeks...months...he would wait patiently for my mother to fall asleep. By the age of ten, he was performing unnatural acts with my body that changed my life forever. My mother was too blind (or pretending to be blind) to see anything. He would take us out to nice restaurants, we go on great family vacations, have family night, sit down at the dinner table together every day...I instantly became his other woman. My mother never said anything because she was so happy. He gave her beautiful gifts, she drove an expensive car and attended exclusive neighborhood meetings—all at the expense of my body. I felt, in my heart, that she knew what my step-father was doing to me. My body began to react differently. I began to vomit in the morning. And three months later, I noticed my stomach began to expand. My step-father never noticed anything. He continued to come in my room every night, but since it was already dark, he didn't notice my growing belly. He was very smart. He convinced my mother to start letting me date boys. My attitude change and I started having mood swings. I hated that man with a passion. For six years of my life I was afraid to tell anyone what this man was doing to my body. I am so sorry, Diary, for dropping tears on your beautiful pages. The tears are causing the ink to run...Good night, Diary...I need to...good night.

Good morning, Diary,

I got a plan. I am going to take all the money I have been saving and leave and never come back. One...two...three...I got about $500. I am going to buy a bus ticket, get a fake ID from one of the boys at school—

Stacy began to breathe hard—

I remember the morning I was planning to leave. I was having breakfast with my mother. I looked across the breakfast table—my mother looked back at me—almost like she wanted to tell me something or apologize for what my step-father has been doing. In the back of my mind, I was thinking about the one o'clock bus schedule I had to make. This was the last time I was ever going to see my mother again. The Devil himself came downstairs, hugged me, kissed my jaw, and told me to have a good day at school. I will never see this man again in my life after today.

I'm sorry, Diary, I just can't stop crying. I feel so cheap and used.

I took my last good look around my house. My mom asked what I was doing...almost like she knew something was going to happen. I said nothing. I waited until she went upstairs, grabbed my back-pack, headed out the door like I was catching the school bus. When no one was looking I ran as fast as I could to the next bus stop.

If you have ever been in this position before, I know the pain has to be unbearable. But I pray that you would ask God to put forgiveness in your heart. Ask him to take away pain, hurt, and suffering that the individual has caused you, so you may be healed and fully recover...so you can enjoy the rest of your life. For some of you, I know it will be hard, but until you do you will never ever be free of that secret. Pray this prayer along with me:

Father, in Jesus Christ of Nazareth name, deliver and set free the man that has destroyed half of my life. Bless him to never hurt another young girl again. Use my life as a testimony to prevent others from letting this happen. Amen.

_____

_____

_____

_____

_____

Chapter 6

My Talk with the Priest

Peter:

"Father, I have a confession."

"What is it my son?"

"I am three generations cursed as a pedophile. My grandfather and father have destroyed lives. And I am in the process of destroying lives. This body of mine has become an instrument of demonic influence, carrying out thoughts that have been whispered to me by Satan himself. I started this act at the age of sixteen. I have committed evil deeds and sinful acts at my home, on my job and several times on family vacation. Loving my wife has become a nightmare. My flesh thirsts like a vampire—a vampire that has pierced the vein on the neck of a human being. I desire sinful pleasures of this wicked world. Father, you still there?"

"Continue, my son."

"I live with a woman who burns hateful passion in my heart toward her. The only reward and benefit that keeps me married is the luxury of my step daughter— who turned me on at the age of seven. Watching her mother give her baths took me into a deep trance. Father, I am a very sick man. Is it possible for God to ever forgive me?"

"Son, God is a forgiving God, but some sins will haunt you all of your life."

"Father, I really believe my wife knows this has been going on for years. But that woman would make any type of sacrifice just to have a fairytale marriage. Father, do you believe me?"

"Son, God knows everything."

"At night, I leave out of the bedroom two to three times a week, about thirty minutes to an hour. I have become a prisoner of the curse that haunts the men in my family. It continues to get more and more uncontrollable. So Father, I have been coming to mass just about all of my life. Going to church with no conviction, assisting with Sunday school with other little boys and girls…Father, I know this probably is one of the most horrible things you have ever heard, but I had to tell someone. The luxury of my step daughter has kept me married to my wife. Father, do you think

I will ever make it to heaven after committing such evil acts?"

"My son, only God knows your future."

"Father, I am so sick. Please help me, Father. Please help me, Father. What should I do?"

The priest began to weep because of the heaviness being told to him. He began to break down.

"A week ago, I drove by a school just to look at the little boys and little girls. Two days ago, I left work early and went to the mall just to feed my addiction. I told my wife I was going to play golf tomorrow, but that is not really what I am going to do. Father, I believe she will continue to sacrifice that little girl until she achieves everything she wants out of life. I remember my dad when I was about ten years old. I was leaving the bathroom but he didn't see me. I noticed he went into my sister's room, so I placed my ear against the wall and I could hear her crying. But I never said or did anything about it. I don't know if it was because of shame or guilt, but I never told a single soul. Now, I am recycling the same sinful seeds. Father, if I die tonight, would I go to hell?"

"Son, if you never confess and ask God's forgiveness, you will go to hell. Son, have you considered any help for this condition of yours?"

"No. I could never tell anyone what I have done."

"Well, son, we need to pray that God will heal, deliver, and set you free from the curse."

"Father, I have a few more things I need to tell you. I have stolen money from my job. I have been to Mexico, across the border, paying thousands of dollars to be intimate with twelve and thirteen year old girls. I raped a girl when I was in college. I have really done some bad things, Father. Just last night I noticed that my step daughter's stomach is getting bigger. So I panicked and this is where I end up when I panic, Father. Father, I just feel so much better. I had to tell someone what I have done in the last six years. I have ruined her life and stolen her innocence in six years. Her body, mind, and soul will never be the same. I have been around so many schools, just looking at the little girls with ponytails, fantasizing...At the bottom of my basement I have hidden secret video tapes. Father, I gotta go. Bye!"

Women that close their eyes to the truth...

Do not be a fool! If you notice your husband has become unattracted to you physically—there is a problem! Innocent people miss opportunities! There is nothing innocent about a step daughter and step father interacting and touching inappropriately. If you have noticed this unacceptable behavior pattern in your marriage—it is already too late. It is time to be pro-active. Thousands of young teenage girls end up in Vegas prostituting and have become a pimp's money making machine. And all at the cost of a mother's selfish and inattentive ways to their daughters.

Hm! Somebody just asked a question...

Contact you local authorities and seek a safe haven for your girl(s). Help keep another girl from selling her soul to the Devil with her body. Continue to ask God for forgiveness for that man. It is imperative that you give your life to Christ now, so the healing process may start. This is not an easy test for any woman and her child. But in your season of deliverance, you will have a testimony to help someone else.

Joe:

"Father, I have sinned against God and against two of his greatest commandments: adultery and fornication. I have become a sex god, under demonic influence, using my body as an instrument of the Devil. Weak, silly women that have not forgiven their husbands, fiancés, boyfriends...Every time I walk in to my condo- a lifestyle of luxury, an environment of exquisite taste- purchased by women that are slaves to sexual desires. Thursday through Saturday, hundreds of women pay just to see me dance erotically. I have so much money that I have a personal fitness trainer to help keep this body in superb conditions. I have slept with married women that married their husbands out of lust, not love. I have danced at bachlorette parties and caused women to call off their weddings. My client list is from the White House to the soccer mom. And at the end of the day, I take a look in the mirror and hate what I have become. I am a slave to women with low self-esteem and no confidence in what they have truly been created to be. I have slept with women who told me they love their husbands, but sold their souls to the Devil—wrestling with demons that have taken control of their minds. All my life I wondered what I would become—and I have become a nightmare. Last night, I slept with a television evangelist's wife. Sometimes I have safe sex, sometimes I don't. Last week I called a married man's house in the suburbs. He answered, such a gentlemen, I advised him I was confirming and doctor's appointment and gave the time and date

I was going to sleep with his wife. Monday I had a wife tell me she told her spouse she had PTA meeting and guess what—I was her PTA meeting.

Father, thank you for being here for me. I have a secret and I have to tell somebody. At the age of fourteen years old, I went to my first boy scout summer camp. And my boy scout leader lived in our neighborhood. He had a beautiful wife, teenage daughters, and a son who was my classmate. One late evening at camp he told me he had a special assignment that would help me earn my stripes in boy scouts. This haunts me everyday of my life. He molested me over and over each night at summer camp. I have been too ashamed to talk to anybody. He changed my life forever. Seven months ago, I went out of town with the CEO of a company for a weekend—a married man with children and a multimillion dollar house. At the price of $5000, I took the job because it was no different from my boy scout leader molesting me. Father, I know I am going to hell when I die. I was raised in a good family with both parents. It makes no difference—you have rich and poor pedophiles... I have been coming to mass every Saturday. I have been infected with AIDS and I am going to give it to as many men and women as I can. I hate this world. I hate God for allowing that to happen to me with my boy scout leader. I will see you Saturday at mass...

Kevin:

"Father, I have sinned against God and the justice system. I have failed families, failed friends, and failed innocent people because of the might dollar. I have paid off people that are in power. I have given checks to experts to come in and plead my case. I have committed perjury over and over again but never gotten caught. I have taught the guilty to become master deceivers to a panel of twelve innocent jurors. I have allowed murderers, child molesters, and doctors with malpractices to get away with crimes they should be serving time for. I have gray streaks of hair from the worry and stress my conscience has caused. I have caused men to walk away without paying alimony. I sold my soul to the Devil for a multimillion dollar house, a 700-Series Mercedes, jewelry, and exclusive vacations. But at the midnight hour, I crawl into my sunken bathtub and I shake and sweat until the sun comes up. I have no more peace. Father, is there any help for a man like me! There is no such thing as an innocent killer.

Fifteen years ago, a CEO of a fortune 500 company paid me two million dollars to get him a not guilty verdict. Father, this man told me a very deep secret and it continues to haunt me after fifteen years. He told me a story—the CEO did—that he planned the perfect murder to kill his beautiful wife and two innocent children, so he could start a life with a Brazilian woman and their new baby. Divorcing his wife was not an option. With a Harvard business degree, finishing top of his class, recognized as

Businessman of the Year on several occasions—he did not have the option to lose his image, wealth, influence, and power. So he paid a hit man to assassinate his family. He had sold his soul to the Devil and made one mistake—that is how I acquired the case. I paid witnesses, experts, and crooked cops—but I know that man killed his family. But because of client-attorney privileges, I could never tell anybody. On Sunday morning we attend the same church. We play golf at the same country club and have even been on vacations together. I pretended nothing ever happened because of the two million he paid me. I coached him and perfected him. When it was time for him to go to court, he was better than me. Just last night, I slept with one of my client's wife. He has no idea she is planning to divorce him and take everything…and I am helping her. To keep us from having a paper trail, she pays her bill with sex. Two years ago, I lied on my taxes, telling the Federal Government that I made two million dollars, when I made close to thirty. I hide my money in offshore accounts and put my accounts in other people's names…

You know, Father, this is a cruel world and sometimes I wonder if God is going to ever come back. I just took this new case for the biggest mob boss in the world. This one is going to get me celebrity status. Hey, Father, did you watch the news about two weeks ago, when a family was assassinated? My client told me he paid to have an undercover cop and his family killed once he found out the cop was an informant. My client had the man killed, his wife killed, his two middle kids and a six month old baby. Father, I just keep representing the scum of the earth. It seems like God made a mistake. The bad people are rich and the good people are poor. I have a problem; I have to stand before a Federal judge that is questioning me about my client. Father, I am telling you now, I am going to lie. I would rather lie to the judge than end up with a bullet in the back of my head. Father, I am starting to feel a little better.

One summer, I was in summer school and I raped one of the coeds. I put on a ski mask. I wore a condom and rubber gloves. And every time I walk into a courtroom and I see her—because she is a prosecutor now—my heart begins to race. Father, is there any help for me? I feel like my life is getting shorter and I am getting deeper....deeper...deeper...

A few months ago, I took a trip down to Vegas and I witnessed a murder. I watched a sixteen-year-old girl get beat to death by her pimp. I was at the wrong place at the wrong time. Every since then I have not been able to get this little girl out of my mind. If I get involved, I will lose my license and practice. If I don't get involved, I will live a miserable life until I die. Father, what shall I do?"

"Son, you have come to the end of the road. It is called a crossroad and there can never be a good ending to this event. You are faced with challenges all of your life. Some of them are self-inflicted, pride and arrogance. My son you have taken, taken, and taken all of your life. This journey you are on is going to lead you to destruction. I suggest that you repent, turn from your wicked ways, and ask God to lead and guide you down the path to righteousness."

"Father, hold that thought. I am getting a text message. This is about my money. Father, I have to go. We will finish this conversation some other time.

Processing the truth...

Processing the truth is one of the hardest things human beings will face in our lives. Separating reality from fantasy...let me give you a simple example of my definitions of reality.

A bill collector calls your home and identifies themselves as a company you owe money to. Then, you acknowledge yourself as someone else but all the time it is really you. It is human nature that we create a personality, an image, a lifestyle that we can not afford, all to impress others that are struggling just like you. Before you leave this world, it is estimated that you will tell thousands of lies. Building without reality makes you lie. And we face these challenges in every area of our lives: spiritually, mentally, financial and decision making.

Second example: marrying for the wrong reason—to fill a void that only God can fill. Driving a car that makes you look good, but you can't afford the payments. Creating a false image with designer clothes, just to be noticed by people that are just like you—subconsciously you are insecure. You are afraid. You hate who you been created to be. You do not have the natural ability to sustain. Your definition to life is being appreciated, being accepted, undiversed conversation that does not create a metaphor for you. Most Americans live in a society that has been created by advertising agents, television commercials, bill boards, news clippings, and your fifteen seconds of glory on My Space. By common nature, we chase smoke dreams that do not exist. God has created, through Jesus Christ, a lifestyle of peace, joy, and happiness. In Him there is no hurt and no pain by loving God with all of your heart, mind, body, and soul. Material things, wealth, promotions, etc…are only tools—not a lifestyle.

Chapter 7

Confessions of Our Thoughts

All men and women have thoughts that are cruel, corrupted, and immoral. It is our private secret, a secret we think no one else knows but us. Take for example:

Scenario A:

A man proposes to his high school sweetheart. He lives on minimum wage. He has a not so sporty vehicle. And he's kind of handsome. He saves all year to buy a ring for the girl of his dreams. He plans for weeks how he his going to propose to the love of his life. So one summer evening he takes her to a romantic picnic. He has a violinist, food prepared by a local chef…At the perfect moment he produces a seashell and gives it to his girl. He hands it to her with the confidence of a lion who rules a kingdom in the forest. His heart is racing, his hands began to shake. As he hands it to her, the music stops and she opens the shell. This little diamond sparkles in the setting sun—she pretends to be happy. She sheds a few tears as she reaches over to give him a fake hug. As she is hugging him, her thoughts began to think evil.

What a little bitty old diamond. And I don't really want to marry him. It has been a cute relationship but it is only temporary. I have bigger and higher dreams planned for my life. This man has fallen in love with me. Now I have to make a decision—hurt him now or hurt him later?

She slowly disconnects from the hug.

If I say yes now, he will celebrate victory. If I say no now, he will break down like a broke puppy.

He gets on his knee as the sun is falling. He looks into her eyes and asked the four words she did not want to hear from him:

"Will you marry me?"

She turns to the left. She turns to the right. She twiddles her thumbs—she couldn't even look him in the eye. And she said....

Scenario B:

My wife just bought me a birthday present. I noticed she had been putting money aside for quite awhile. She enters the house. She approached me on my big day and said:

"Honey, how are you doing today? Today is your birthday! I didn't plan you a surprise birthday party. I didn't plan an extravagant dinner...but I noticed a few months ago while we were shopping that you looked at some different things...so, I would like you to close your eyes and I will be right back with your present."

She left the room and returned a few moments later with a nice size box. She has a little help from our son because it was a heavy box. I slowly unwrapped my present and I noticed it was a new set of golf clubs—the cheap ones. I pretended to be happy, gave her a hug and a kiss—you know how we do it. I just put on a little show for her. She walked away as confident as a wife could be. But she had no idea that I still had an empty void from my present. These cheap ugly golf clubs...as soon as I can get that receipt I am taking them back. She wasted a whole bunch of time and money for nothing. I am going to wait a week, and then I am taking them back. I'm going to add some more money and buy the ones I really want. She will never know the difference...

It's Sunday morning. I can not believe how she came to church dressed...that ugly dress...all that weave in her head....and those fake contacts...and she has the nerve to think she is all that...she needs to sit her Jezebel-self down...Why did I come to church this morning?

"Good morning, boss, how are you?"

...With those wrinkled pants on. Wifey should have helped him...ooh and his breath stinks...

"Ok, boss, I am heading to work. Have a good day!"

I wish this checkout line would move faster...she acts like I have all day...then had the nerve to think she is cute in all of that make up...with her dumb self...

"Look, honey, how do you like my new dress?"

"Aw...it's nice, dear..."

You look like the granny off of the Hillbillies.

"Hey, Mom."

"Hey, Son."

I am going to have to set her straight. Somebody has to tell Mom she is getting old and she is not a young chick anymore. She is forgetting she is a grandmother...wanting to be young....

"Honey, did you pay the credit card bills?" she asked.

"Yes, dear!" he responded.

"Why isn't the balance going down?"

She just keeps spending! She makes me sick! Then she has the nerve to say she is paying the bills...She needs to sit herself down...

"Mary, how do you like my new dress?"

"Well, it's not really you..."

She is never going to get a man dressed like that...squeezing in those little tight dresses...

"Hi, Tom and Laurie."

Hm...I really like his wife. He has no idea...with her fine self. He acts like he doesn't want her...Baby, don't you see I want you? I wish I could tell her I want her...

"I will be your waitress this afternoon. Can I take your order?"

I want her to leave right now...with her ugly self...why do I always get the ugly waitresses? She needs to fix her hair...

"Ma'am, we only have one pair of shoes left in that size."

I do not need all this attitude. I am spending my money. If I was not buying these shoes, she would not have a job...with her ugly self...she must be jealous because I can afford shoes and she can't...

"Ok daughter it's time to go to bed, no calls after nine."

I can't stand you! You just keep on ruining my life! I can't wait until I am 18 and be on my own... be my own woman. This woman, all she is concerned abut is herself and dad, that's all. She never cares about the things I like to do...

"Did you have a good time, dear? I really enjoyed the restaurant we went to, the service was good and the environment was friendly. I really had a pleasant time."

This was the worst date I have ever been on. He just rambled his mouth, the food was not good, the environment was not friendly...Ugh! But I can't tell him the truth it would devastate him...

"Did you like the house I showed you, ma'am? It's in a real good neighborhood, friendly community, nice schools..."

Hell, no! This is the ugliest house that this woman has ever shown us.

"Man, if you don't tell me the truth, me and the kids are leaving. I am going to ask you one more time, did you have sex with her?"

Yes, I did. Do you think I will tell you the truth? Do I look like a fool? But I really had a good time.

"Honey, I just can't stop thinking a bout something. Every time I look at my son, he looks different than all my other kids. Is this my son? I need t know…"

No! But I needed help paying my bills so I blamed you…but you will never know the truth.

"Hi, mom! Thought I would stop over and bring the new guy in my life, will you be home after six?

"Yes dear, stop on by…"

Ding dong!

"Hi, mom, this is Jim. This is the guy I have been telling you about….the guy that has changed my life….

Your momma is fat and ugly. She needs Jenny Craig!

"Are you pregnant?"

I'm just telling you yes so I can marry you, then I will pretend I lost the baby...you fool...

"Man, I hate you!"

What you don't know is that I hate you too...with your ugly self...

Every year millions of people have thoughts, conversation, interaction... whether it's the telephone, texting, or socializing. We have been put into a box because we are so afraid to tell someone the truth. So we will live this lie and deal with an unreal relationship, camouflaged by smoke illusions in mirrors. We say one thing but we think differently. In order to have a healthy relationship with anybody—male or female, adult or young adult—we must learn to communicate. We cannot be in bondage or so afraid of losing someone that we begin to build a false relationship. Marriages take place every hour around the world. Most marriages are built on lies because we play games with people to obtain things for our own personal lives. We conceal the truth so we can fulfill our selfish rewards. But as time lapses, eventually the true person will come to the forefront. We have destroyed the lives of those closest to us. Gossip magazines entice us to manipulate people. Television teaches us to play house in marriages that have no love. Songs make us think about people we wish we had in our lives. The internet takes us on search engines...trying to fall in love with someone through online love connections.

But it's so easy to start building a life on biblical principles and a biblical foundation. The Lord focuses on living a life of truth because Jesus Christ represents the truth. If you struggle telling friends and family the truth, ask Christ to help you to start telling the truth. Don't be controlled by evil thoughts of the devil that whisper these things to your mind. Don't be pressured and controlled by the lifestyle of

the world that drives you to live in a fantasy world—
a lifestyle built on fashion, body image, and a prosperous lifestyle. Everyday that you are able to wake
up and practice telling the truth to the people that you
love is going to build a solid foundation in your life.
And you should never say never. Telling the truth
is the first sign of allowing Christ to fill your heart.
Rather it's in the grocery store, among coworkers,
family reunion, or just having a drive with friends.
You can't erase the past but I challenge you to a new
beginning. A beginning filled with growth, maturity,
accountability, acceptance of the truth and a world
free from bondage. As I close this chapter, you should
have a new beginning of communicating. Next time
you tell a lie, ask yourself, why?

Chapter 8

Why?

This is a big word used everyday of our lives: **Why**? But today, you are about to go on a different journey, a journey that will change your life forever. A journey where men and women have made bad choices due to a decrease in finances, their home is too small, or a choice of having to ride in a smaller car because they could not afford the minivan. Some are just too lazy to make sacrifices and adjustments to save a life. I am talking about when a man or woman plays God, by taking the life through a process called abortion.

Every five minutes around the United States a baby is aborted. This is the decision of a man or woman who failed to take responsibility at the time that this wonderful human being was created. Unplanned pregnancies…families that are of good statute…private school, Christian schools, those in the suburbs, grandparents—all whisper off to clinics in the midnight hour. They drive at night to avoid embarrassment and disgrace in front of their community. This is option used by wives who have became pregnant in unfaithful relationships, teenage girls who have been molested or raped by their father figures, etc... Mothers have made decisions based on a young lady's academic outcome instead of responsibility of raising a baby. We have actually played God: we created a life and then we took a life.

So as I take you on this journey I want your greatest imagination to come to the forefront. You are about to meet some of the most incredible human beings in the world. You stole their destiny, stole their purpose, stole their creativity, and stole love and courtship. You stole their opportunities of smelling and seeing the creations of God—just because it was an inconvenience to your life.

Okay you ready? Let's go!

You have to go on a spiritual journey with me because this will pull you out of your comfort zone. These are angels writing to their parents who aborted them...letters from heaven.

To Lora:

Hi, Mom and Dad, just writing you this letter form heaven. I had a talk with God today. And He taught me a very valuable lesson about forgiveness. He said in order for me to remain an angel and remain in heaven, I have to forgive you and dad. So I am starting my letter off by saying, I forgive you for rewriting my life. You made a choice without my input. You both killed me. But I have just learned to forgive. I was a very handsome little boy. I will never be able to be a husband one day or have a wife… you just stole my life! You never gave me a chance to experience daycare. As I look down from heaven and see all the beautiful children playing, crying, sucking bottles… Today I watched a little boy ride his first bike and I began to cry. He had a red bike with a red helmet. His Dad was so proud of him. Dad, you never gave me a chance for you to be proud of me! You convinced yourself that having me was not a good idea. I wonder what it would feel like to get a hug and kiss from Mom…well you know. But I still love you both. I hung out with Jesus today and He taught me a valuable lesson about love. I learned that He paid the biggest sacrifice for mankind. I will never have the opportunity to meet you unless one day you make it to heaven. And I will be a little boy standing by Jesus, blond hair and blue eyes. And I will run up to you and Mom and give you a big hug because I forgive you.

*If you are thinking about having an abortion, the answer should be **no** without a second thought. You may make a decision that will change your life forever by killing an unborn baby. You may have killed the next president of the United States of America. How do you live with that? That image will burn into your mind forever.*

To Susan:

Hi, Mommy! You made this decision all alone because you don't even know who my Dad is. But I do! I'm just up in heaven walking about looking down at you. I cried today, just to see all the Mom's that were shopping with their little girls, calling them princess...I wonder what a dress would look like on me. In heaven we wear robes. I ran across someone about a week ago and I found out that he is my brother! I told him I would write a letter for both of us. Mom, you can't just keep having all these abortions! You allowed that doctor and all those pamphlets to convince you that I wasn't created yet. But, Mom, I was a living spirit. And God had placed my spirit in your womb. I was looking forward to my ponytails. I was looking forward to spilling milk and making a mess, running through the house... I wonder what pampers feel like but you never gave me a chance. Well, your son—he loves you too....we both love you. Jesus Christ taught us that we have to forgive you and love you. We are doing fine. We are in heaven hanging out with God and all His angels.

And we have a section with millions of babies where Moms and Dads have made the decision to kill the unborn baby. I have a lot of fun but I would have loved the opportunity to be human. Mom, you stole my life from me. I never had a chance to have a boyfriend, never had the chance to wear a designer wedding gown. I would have liked you to make my prom dress and take me shopping for all my accessories. Mom, what does a peanut butter and jelly sandwich taste like? I watch millions of kids all over the world enjoy peanut butter and jelly sandwiches. I look down and I wondered what having a baby doll would be like...but you stole that part of my life too. I will never have a baby doll. My brother and I... we are always praying for you to give your life to Christ so we can visit you in heaven. I'm a very beautiful girl and my brother is very handsome. Mom, you have to take better care of yourself. You have to make decisions because you are destroying your body every time you allow the doctors to do an abortion. One day you are going to fall madly in love and you will try to have a baby. But, God is not going to bless you. Oops! Mom I have to go. I hear the sounds of the trumpet. We are both apart of Heaven's youth choir and we are headed to practice.

Ps. We love you! I'll be the little girl with my little brother standing by the pearly white gates. We will be waiting for you.

Letter to Stacy:

Hi, Mom and Dad. I hate both of you! You have totally destroyed my purpose. I had inside of me the cure for cancer! But you and Dad killed my purpose. So, I want you to know that your son was going to help change and save millions of lives. But, you wanted to play god. When I first came to heaven I would just cry myself to sleep. And over time my cries began to get shorter and I began to hate both of you. So one day I had a knock at my door. My big bother name Jesus took a walk with me. He said,

"Little man, they beat me with thirty-nine lashes, beat me until I was unrecognizable, hung me on the cross and began to drive nails in my hands and feet... but I had to forgive them. I don't agree with what your parents did, but I had to forgive the whole world of their sins. You only have to forgive two people. So the very moment you began to forgive those who destroyed your life, I will begin to heal your broken heart. What I would like you to do is to pray for them every night. And ask my Father to fix their hearts so they never do this again. And one day you will see them walk through those beautiful golden gates, because of your prayers."

Mom and Dad, I just want you to know that I love you now because of that talk I had with my big brother Jesus Christ. Sometimes I look down from heaven and I wish I had a red fire truck. I wish I was able to be strapped in the car seat and go on long rides with Dad. I think about what it would have been like to go to my prom and asked you to borrow your cool sports car, Dad. So the next time you get pregnant, Mom, keep the baby—that way we can all be in heaven together. You know what? I really like race cars also, Dad, but I will never have the chance to play with one. One more thing and I have to say, because I want to be free. The night that you both decided that an abortion was cheaper than having me, I heard the arguing back and forth. I heard Mom talking about not wanting anymore babies. I could hear those things in her womb and I just wanted her to know that. I was a living spirit and I was alive and well, just waiting for my body to form. Mom, the next time you are riding in the car, turn the radio down because you listen to the music too loudly. Well its time to go, I may write you again I may not...we'll see...

Your little boy from heaven that loves you....

To Donna:

Hi Mom! Guess what, you killed your only set of twins you were ever going to have! But you didn't know we were twins. It would have been one of the coolest things to ride in our dual stroller...her in the front and me in the back. Guess what, we are identical. We look just alike! They have given us the coolest robes in heaven, and we still dress like twins. Today we were walking down the golden road being escorted by Peter. Have you ever read the story about Peter, Mom? He is one of coolest disciples. He was teaching us about his journey on earth and the experiences he had with our big brother Jesus. He was teaching us about not telling lies. So, Mom, I heard you when I was in your womb. I heard you tell Dad that you weren't pregnant. Why would you do that? You chose just to kill both of us? We would hear you when you went to the club Mom, dancing to all the music, we could hear all of that. And you have to change your eating habits. Some of food you gave us wasn't the best, Mom. We love you! We wish we had a chance to meet you and hug you and be there to help you. But you took our lives when you decided to have an abortion. Every once in awhile we look down and pray for you. Sometimes I don't want to pray for you. I will never be able to celebrate a birthday. I always wondered what ice cream tasted like and how cool it would be to run in the sand barefooted. You never allowed our future to manifest. Did you know we were both going to be doctors? We were both going to have our own practice. I was going to be the one to perform surgeries. Later on in life you will end up with breast cancer...but now someone else is going to have to perform that surgery. I've been praying for you...Ooh, about 2 weeks ago we were sitting down talking with Jesus and He taught us about how much He loved His mother Mary. She was such a wonderful and good mother...I would have loved being in the kitchen watching you cook so I could cook for my own husband. Mom, some nights I watch you twist and turn as thoughts of the abortion bother you. Jesus taught us how to pray a special prayer for you. After you receive this letter, we will pray for you to have perfect peace. We love you, Mom. Mom, you know one day we will be waiting for you. We pray that you turn your life around and allow Jesus to come into your life. So that when you die you can come to heaven. Heaven is one of the coolest places, and I came when I was just a little bitty baby, not even 2 weeks old. All the wonderful angels have taken good care of us. Well Mom, its time for choir rehearsal. I hope by the time you receive this letter your life will be changed....

From both of us with love,
Your little girls

Karen:

Hi, Mom. Today, Mom, was not a good day. I was looking down at earth and I saw a very beautiful yellow dress. I wonder what it would be like for you to take me shopping and buy a dress for your little princess. But you and dad made a very bad choice by aborting me before I was created into a human being. Mom, do you think about me? Do you wonder about what it would be like if you would have had me? What kind of relationship we would have had? Do you ever stop and think…stare off into space at work and think about the bad decision you have made? You took my life! You are actually murderers, you and dad. Today I had an opportunity to hang out with one of the disciples named Peter. He taught me a very valuable lesson about being able to forgive the people we love. Peter is my big brother in heaven. He checks on me and everyday he comes by and encourages me. He taught me a lesson about forgiving you and Dad. You didn't know that one day when I grew up that I was going to be a great school teacher. I was going to help develop young minds to be great leaders. Several of my students would have become governors, mayors, senators…or even presidents of United States. I hope you receive this letter with love knowing that I had to tell you the truth. Next time you see Dad, tell him I'm praying for him. Now that I have forgiven you, my life is beginning to take a new direction. I love you more now than I ever did in my life, because here in heaven you have to forgive people to live with God. So every night before you go to bed take a look outside and look up in the sky…you might see an angle that might be your little girl…well I have to go now…off to choir rehearsal. I hope to write back to you real soon…

P.S. Mom, never have an abortion again in your life, you never know who you are killing...

Your little girl...

Dealing with the truth

Dealing with truth may cause you to cry, feel sorry for yourself, or even make you suicidal. But you have to acknowledge the truth so you can begin a healing process. I am not the judge or the jury. Only God can judge you on Judgment Day. I only want to raise the awareness so you are able to make better choices in life. Abortions, destroying a life, are not the way to deal with the situation. Most states across the nation have given you a way to deal with this a better way. You can drop the baby off at a fire station or police station or local church or put the baby up for adoption. At least give the baby the opportunity to change the world. Never let financial stability cloud your judgment. Don't let the fact that love is not in the relationship or being judged by others because you are unmarried be the reason you have an abortion. If you are ever put in this position, only allow the decision to be based on a life or death situation.

Now, for you mothers that have already committed abortions, here is a little pray that I pray for God to begin to heal you heart, mind, and soul:

Dear God,
Forgive me because I have sinned against you. I made a bad choice without consulting you. I know

that your darling son Jesus Christ died on the cross for my sins. I am asking you to show me mercy and grace and that you will never close my womb, that I am able to give birth. I take full responsibility for my actions; I blame no one but myself. Can you please fill this void that I have for a baby I never knew? Give me peace and give me joy and a better understanding with your strength through the word, that you may guide me...thanking you in advance for forgiving me for all my sins through JESUS CHRIST, Amen.

Kathy:

I should not even call you mom...you're the woman that destroyed my basketball career. I was going to be the next Michael Jordan! And all your financial problems would have been over. But you couldn't make an 18 year commitment. All your dreams would have come to pass, Mom. And you would have had an opportunity to see your son enjoy the game of basketball. But no! You decided to follow my dad who convinced you not to have me because of his financial obligations. Because of that decision, you aborted me. I will never play t-ball, never play elementary, middle school, or high school ball because of your decision... I was going to lead Charlotte, North Carolina to a national basketball championship. I was going to hit the winning game shot at the buzzer...But! You stole my victory, Mom. Today I was walking down these beautiful golden roads in heaven. And I ran across a man named Solomon, are you familiar with him, Mom? He was a great king that led his people to victory. But he taught me also a very valuable lesson about loving and forgiving and about honesty. Living in heaven requires me to love unconditionally, be honest and be accountable for my actions. But I hated you for a long time. But today is a new day with a new beginning. I will live out all my days in heaven with God and Jesus and all my big brothers. So I am writing this to tell you that I forgive you for taking my life. I forgive dad for convincing you to take my life. I will be the little boy standing by the golden gate. I will have number 7 on my jersey.

Ps. Love you.

Letter to Joe:

You may be wondering who's writing you this letter. You never knew me or heard mention of me, but I am the son you never knew about. You may remember spending that one Saturday night with that beautiful woman. You did not know she would become pregnant and have an abortion without ever telling you. I never blamed you for this but I always wondered what it would be like to have a Dad of my own. Looking down from heaven, I noticed this beautiful red and white fire truck in the window of a store. Dad, I wish that you could have bought that for me for my birthday. But you see, Dad, I was never born. I missed so many opportunities for piggy back rides, taking the training wheels off my bike, attending my first major league baseball game and eating a foot long hot dog. I look just like you Dad, blond hair blue eyes…About this time I guess you are feeling very angry over a decision that was made without your control. I wish Mom would have had an honest line of communication with you. You know I watch you go to work every day and I am always praying for you. I pray one day you would accept Jesus Christ into your life so you can come to heaven and bring me that fire truck. Dad! I noticed you are a sports fan…last Sunday you were watching the super bowl you were cheering and rooting for your favorite team. It would have been nice to be there screaming and running through the house, cheering when you cheerer, but Mom stole that from both of us. I'm asking you to find it in your heart to forgive her. Why she made this decision I don't know. I always wanted to just be a human little boy, run up and down football fields, while fans cheered me on, or even swing a bat and hit a homerun....but she had no idea, I was going to be a great race car driver. She stole my dream. Today I hung out with Matthew. He is one of the disciples that worked with Jesus Christ over 3000 years ago. He taught me a very valuable lesson about forgiving, so now I have learned to forgive Mom for the bad decision she made. The next time you see her if you could give her a big hug and kiss I would appreciate it.

Ps. I will be waiting at those golden gates for you, Dad. By the way, bring me a baseball!

Your little boy

Letter to Darryl:

Darryl, this is your little girl and my name is December. You never met me. And you probably never will. When you were 16 years old you dated your high school sweetheart. She became pregnant and one Friday night her parents decided to take her to a clinic. They felt she was too young to be a parent and raise a baby, but the real truth— my grandparents did not want to make the necessary sacrifices. They were proud, felt ashamed about what the neighbors would say...the community and even the church. So my grandparents decided to just kill me by making my mom have an abortion. She was only 17. They had no idea I would grow up and be a great astronaut. They would have been very proud of me. But all three of them killed my dream. I really have a cool name –December. John the Baptist gave me that name. The reason my name is December because it was the month Jesus Christ was born in Bethlehem. It's also the month all the little boys and girls celebrate Christmas. I love you, Dad. Looks like you are losing hair off the top of your head, there's a bald spot… you should slow down when you are driving to and from work. One day I saw you run a red light and you got pulled over by a cop on a motorcycle that gave you a ticket. You became angry and frustrated but that is the price you pay when you break the law. Sometimes I just cry because I wanted you to be able to one day walk me down the aisle and give me away to my Prince Charming. I don't fault you but I do fault my mom and grandparents. Everyday I wonder what it would be like to just have the opportunity to play with other girls, make dolls, bake cakes, or even design clothes. Well Dad, it's time once again as I end this letter. I want you to know I will pray for you everyday…in heaven. I may write you back, but I don't want to make any promises.

Ps. Dad, just go buy you a little wig and put it on top of that bald spot.

Letter for Kevin:

Stupid! I guess you are wondering why I would call you that. I called you that because you are stupid for giving a woman five hundred dollars to kill your baby. You are very selfish. You have low self esteem, no personal integrity. You should not call yourself a man. You chose to just kill me instead of taking responsibility. For a long time my pillow was drenched with tears of sadness and heartbreak. My heart is full of anger and bitterness and resentment toward a man I never knew. You paid five hundred dollars to kill me! As you begin to read this letter, I want you to know, I was going to be one of the greatest golf players in the world, better than Tiger Woods... but you stole my dream, Dad. I saw Mom about a couple weeks ago. She was sitting at home in a corner balled up in a knot because she had found a receipt from when she paid for the abortion. She wondered...thought... She knew it would be my birthday. She just cried and cried until she cried herself to sleep. Look at what you did! If you had been a man instead of a little boy, I would be playing and jumping, dating girls and enjoying my life. I was walking around in heaven with God and He was teaching me a very special lesson about forgiving. He taught me about how He had to forgive all the people that mistreated His son—even the people that took His life. The love He had for those people was unconditional. So I was convicted, ashamed, and I felt so embarrassed as I walked around holding God's hand...I began to weep in sorrow and my heat began to heal, the hurt began to leave. So now I am able to write this letter to tell you that I love you and I forgive you. And I pray that you would give your life to Christ one day, so you can make it to heaven. And I will be the little boy with the golf bag, waiting for you.

Love,
Your baby boy, forever

Letter to Mark:

Cry baby! Dad, you are nothing but a crybaby. All you ever do is wine, wine, wine, you crybaby. We are triplets; it's me and my siblings here. You have killed all three of us, you crying baby. You are nothing but a Momma's boy. You allowed your Mom to convince you to pay money for our mother to abort us. That old witch, with her old self. You allowed the devil to get inside your mind and convince you that now is not the time for you to have any kids. We were going to be the best things to ever happen to her. She was too proud and arrogant to have grandchildren born out of wedlock. She was more concerned about what friends and family thought. So you have missed the most awesome three little girls... we were going to love you, nurture you and be there for you as you became older in life. But to live in heaven you have to have a forgiving heart, mind, body and soul. We were taught through our big brother Jesus Christ that in order to stay in heaven and live with the angels, we had to forgive. So as hard as this is for me, Dad, I have to forgive you and my grandmother for making the worst choice that both of you have ever made in your life. Me and my siblings pray daily for your peace and happiness. Be encouraged the next time you have been given a blessing—a child. You know how cool it would have been for all of us to be on a five-seater...you, Mom behind you, and us three girls...we would have had our helmets on, knee and elbow pads...just to be on the safe side. Dad, could you ever imagine, all three of us would have gotten married at the same time and you would have given us all away at the same time on the same day...how awesome! Well, next time you see Mom, tell her we are praying for her and we love her. Because I have decided to forgive you, I would have been your favorite girl. Ok Dad it's time to go. Receive this letter with love!

From your girls

Unconditional love

All through life, as a man and woman, you are going to be forced to make some uncomfortable decisions, decisions that may change your life forever. You have to set a path and make that path a beautiful journey. When you marry and become one with your spouse, it is unconditional. Love should be based on endurance through the roughest times in life. You should come together as an awesome man and woman created to give life and help change and redirect mankind. At what point in your life do you decide to own up to every wrong choice and decision you made without Godly consulting? Finances should never be an excuse—over extended credit cards is not an excuse. Love not in the relationship is not an excuse. People-pleasing and worrying about how others judge you can not be excuses. There is no such thing as an unplanned marriage or unplanned pregnancy. It is never an excuse to say, o*ops we made a mistake*. Millions of women all over the United States spend millions of dollars trying to become pregnant. I'm not trying to be thee judge or the jury, but a baby is a gift from God. Whether it has been 24 hours or it has been 9months, it is still a human being no matter what form! It is given life first through the Spirit of God. It becomes a living soul. God breathes life into a mother's womb and that is a blessing. Marriages are destroyed because of these decisions; marriages are built because of these decisions. The next time you engage in making a decision on taking a life—I challenge you to stand before a jury and explain to them why you killed an innocent baby.

Chapter 9

Rent, why buy?

Men and women stay in relationships for years, then all of as sudden, the love has vanished into someone else's heart. The bank account has been depleted, and you take a look in the mirror and say to yourself, *"where is this heading?"* And by the time you have made that statement, one of the parties involved in the relationship has moved on with their life and you end up with an empty bag. So, you feel abandoned, deserted, and betrayed. You feel mentally and physically used. That person you had puppy love with, has risen to the occasion and started a new life—disappearing with all the hard work you have into that person to make them great. Now someone else benefits from it! So, women who settle for less while waiting for Mr. Right, you would rather compromise the standard set inside of you because of your age, beauty, and your resources. You just became a common woman, settling for whatever you could get. Every year men and women commit suicide over a broken heart. Your heart walked out the door with a person you never knew.

You know what, don't let it be you☺

In the mix of playing house, created by a fragment of weak imaginations, a lust baby is created. She thought by getting pregnant this man would marry her, commit to her, and devote his life to being a father and a husband. But it's all a fairytale! Years go by and she ends up having two to three lust babies only to find out she was nothing but a rented relationship.

Okay, I want to share a quick story with you. The names have been changed to protect the innocent:

Two years ago a very attractive, energetic, outgoing, 'I have a dream', young lady walked into the club. Her appearance made everything freeze in the club. She was a well dressed masterpiece, but only one man could get her attention. He was suave, intelligent, a gentleman; a man of integrity that totally swept her off her feet. His eyes hypnotized her; put her into a daze where she forgot her own name. As they began exchange words, smiles, gentle touches, she knew that this was the man of her life. Instantly her dreams and drive were put on hold all in the name of love.

A few days after meeting him, she could not stop talking about the man that had swept her off her feet. Her girlfriends would smirk with jealousy, because they could see the dazzle in her eyes as this man began to breathe life into her. They finally decided to go out on their first date. He asked when he could see her. One afternoon he decided to stop by just to bring her one red rose with a small card signed *I just can't get you off my mind*. She became weak in the knees; her voice trembled as words fell out of her mouth. She looked him into the eyes and said, "Make me a promise you will never hurt me." Being the gentleman he was, he reached down to give her a very snuggly hug and said, "All my life I have been searching for someone to fill the other half of my heart." He kissed her on the cheek and told her goodnight.

Over the course of three months, they were the perfect couple. She was so confident that he was the one. She decided to move in his apartment. Another three months later she has some very exciting news. She waited one evening, prepared a candlelight dinner and lit candles all over the room. She had soft music playing and she was dressed very provocatively when he walked in. She grabbed his briefcase and escorted him to the dinner table. She began to serve the food she spent all day preparing. He described his work day; she blushed and blew him kisses.

After the wonderful dinner she handed him a beautifully wrapped box. He blushed with excitement like a kid on Christmas morning. His heart began to race as he tore the box open. Inside there was a pink baby bottle. He began to cry, got up, and gave her a big hug. "I am so happy!" he exclaimed.

Over the next nine months their lives would be an incredible journey. Everything a woman could want for a new born baby, he provided for her. He proved to be a hidden diamond, lost in the world set aside just for her.

As she progressed in her pregnancy, she became more and more excited. Having a new baby and her dream man—her life would never be the same. But deep in the back of her mind, she was surely convinced he would propose to her. Unfortunately, she was caught up with the glitz and glamour of the relationship that she didn't say anything. But that small voice continued to torment her day after day with: *will he marry me or will he not?*

Early one Saturday morning, she began to feel contractions. He was sound asleep but as she shifted and turned in the bed, he woke out of his sleep. He reached to comfort her. She said, "I feel great pain." It being her first pregnancy, she was very paranoid. He called the doctor and described her symptoms. The doctor advised it was time to deliver the baby. She had packed very special bag months before the baby was due. He reached in the closet, grabbed the bag, and they whispered off into the night. About seven a.m., Sunday morning, a brand new baby girl was birthed into the world. She was eight pounds, nine ounces, twenty-seven inches long. It was like God himself or like a stork dropped her off.

Instantly, their lives began to spiral downward. She became more attentive to the baby and he became more attentive to making money. His warm words became fewer...he began to drift into his own world. Engagement was getting further and further away. Twelve months later, she was pregnant again.

Now she had put on excessive weight so she was no longer slim line figured. She was a woman who had given birth to two beautiful babies. Her confidence began to dwindle away. She noticed that the guys were no longer paying attention to her like they did before she became pregnant...before she fell for the man of her dreams. Her hope of having a beautiful wedding seemed to ride off in the midnight hour, never to return. He began to make more excuses for not taking her out to dinner and spending quality time with her. The only true joy that he ever had was with his two children, who he spent most of his free time with on his days off.

On their second year anniversary of being the "perfect couple"—thought by friends, relatives, and associates—she decided to have an anniversary party and invite all their friends. She pulled out all the stops, expecting this turn their relationship around. She made the appropriate arrangements, had both kids dropped off at her mom's and began her journey around seven a.m. She stopped at the beauty shop, got her a very fly hairstyle, got her nails dazzled up. Her next stop was her favorite store to buy a stunning dress. She had put on four to five dress sizes from the first time she met him (she went from a seven to a twelve). So, she looked and looked until she finally found a dress that she thought gave her the best definition. She stopped by the jeweler and picked up the chain she had purchased for him. She found the perfect bottle of wine and headed back home. She became very sad as the day began to dwindle down and he had not called her all day. The guest began to arrive around six thirty. The part was set to start at seven thirty. A lot of his friends and coworkers began to socialize, mingle, interacting with one another.

Around nine fifteen, her man's best friend showed up with some disturbing news. He had come to relay that, unfortunately, her man was not coming home. His best friend felt very uncomfortable as he looked into the eyes of the mother, who had carried both of his friend's children. She asked why, but he refused to get into a long conversation. As she slowly waked out of the room, tears fell down her face because she suddenly knew that someone else was in his life.

About three pm the next day, he finally came home. She could smell the woman's fragrance that rushed through the house. He slowly walked into the bedroom and over to the crib. He picked up the baby and sat down in the rocking chair. He began to rock and sing to the baby. Earlier that morning as she sat down with the baby, she recognized that this man's love for her was gone and would never come back.

I have let two years of my life go up and down like a yo-yo...playing house. Month after month, I noticed he started getting home later. The last month he spent more time and love with the kids than he did with me.

Every night, over the last year, I have been going to bed on a wet pillow drenched with the tears from my eyes. The man I have loved with all my heart, mind, body, and soul was the worst mistake I ever made in my life. I have allowed this man to play house! He never had any intentions of marrying me. I was only rent for hire.

Lude 1: Strong women make homes!

A strong woman of God makes a home for her family.

Huuuhhh...just breathe...

A strong woman focuses first on pleasing others not herself. Here is a woman who was rent for hire for two years of her life. She was paralyzed by a ring; an engagement ring that actually created a false illusion. She was hoping one day to become a married woman. So, as you go on in your life, you will learn: nothing for yourself. Take the time to ask yourself, if I build a home for a family and not myself, can I be a very happy woman?

At the beginning of time God created one man for one woman. They were created to share an experience that would last a life time. But most people take advantage of other people because of impure motives...in other words, "what can you do for me?" So, here is a woman that played house for two years without a purpose. She entrapped herself into a fantasy that was created by pleasing people that did not love her. She had an impressive conversation, talking about a man that only had one purpose: a temporary relationship.

Just because you have an engagement ring, does not mean that man is going to marry you. It could possibly be a trick of the Devil to detour you from your first and true love. So, the next time you are faced with making a decision—either to play house or make a home—make your decisions based on biblical principles and the true Word of God. Consecrate yourself by staying pure and holy until you say the most beautiful words out of your mouth: I do. By engaging in sexual activity and false intimacy, you have built a relationship guaranteed to fail because it is built on lust not love.

A real woman would first focus on building a home to please God. She builds a family to please God, has kids to please God, and even gets married to please God—nothing for herself. The Word of God says, when a man finds a wife, he finds a good thing, and obtains favor from the Lord. So, you depreciate your value as a good thing when you engage in sexual activity before marriage. You have been given a place where God will honor you through your husband and through your children. Slow down! Don't allow time to control you! You can control time with God. You are not getting older. You are still as beautiful as the day you were created in your mother's womb through the eyes of God. And in time, God will send your perfect mate; the one God has molded and shaped to create happiness, joy and peace with God and you. Why settle for second best? Why continue to divorce over and over again? The pressure of the world forces you to make decisions on temporary illusions created by Satan himself.

I believe God has not forgotten about you. Continue to pray, maintain, and prepare yourself for the man God is about to send for you—at His time. Don't panic, don't panic! God has not forgotten about you! I don't care how many weddings you may attend. Do not envy or become jealous of someone else's blessings. Your time could be right around the corner.

Somebody just asked the question: Why has god delayed my spouse? The problem is not your spouse; the issue is that God has to prepare *you* to become married. Being a submissive wife is a job. It is not easy having someone lead your life. You may rebel, retaliate, and you may even decide not to be intimate with your husband because of your immature and childish ways. These are the ways of your mother, grandmother, and other failed marriages. All of them are women who have become bitter, misguided, and have no life. So, now you can see my point on how important it is to be a strong woman—you can build a strong family.

Proverbs 31 describes the virtuous woman of God. Life is not just about having children as an accessory or to impress coworkers, friends, and associates—its being able to build young soldiers for the Kingdom. You have to be able to nurture them from one month until the age of eighteen years old. It will require a lot of sacrifice, restless nights, bills being delayed, your wardrobe versus their wardrobe, and not always having the right answer for your children. We live in a society where it is so easy for you to take your children to the neighbors, daycare, sleepovers, grandparent's house, and even leave them with church members and all so you can make time for your selfish, immature life. You would rather get a manicure, spend four hours in the beauty salon, and window shop for eight hours, than to take the time to read the Word of God to your children. You are probably too mad to continue reading this book, but the truth will make you free. Once again, I am not trying to be a judge or jury. I am only removing the band aid from soar spots in your life; a spot you have conveniently hidden for years.

Now, let's focus on Mr. Right. Looking for Mr. Right is going to cost you commitment and a relationship with Jesus Christ. He will help lead you and guide you down the path of righteousness that comes with a guarantee. True happiness in a marriage can only be made up of a relationship with Jesus Christ.

Lude 2: Weak women play house

Why would you play house with a man that only God can change? Millions of women have tried to influence men with sex and manipulation, but have never been able to keep a man to themselves. If I had to take a survey, I believe, as a result, that in fifty percent of marriages the women are playing house. There is no truth in communication and no truth about the children. Finances cause mates to be led into adulterous relationships just to find relief.

Playing house was created to avoid committing to each other in wedlock. It is so easy to pretend to be happy, live a fantasy life, and to avoid dealing with the truth. Instead you should just say, "I don't want to marry you." But we pretend it is okay for us to live in adultery and fornication—with relationships that will one day come to an end. We will leave behind a closed chapter in a relationship; a relationship that was started with no intentions of creating an ending. Next, the blame game has been put in motion. This results in financial burdens, children born of lustful moments, and rolling the dice to see who gets what. Then, one day you are staring out of the window looking at a life that has been created in havoc and destroyed by Satan himself.

Playing house is a common term used by little children. These children create a fantasy world with make-believe characters. So many women create make-believe characters, acting out their fantasies through a relationship built on lies. The man has no intentions of marrying the woman. So, she becomes a victim of her own lies in her make-believe world. She has placed herself on a pedestal having no idea that death will be the end result.

Let's identify the word death. In this instance, I'm referring to a dead end relationship that will not have a happy ending. A woman is forced to take her illegitimate children into a new environment and a new relationship. Now, this woman has become the product of another failed relationship.

Someone may ask this question to themselves: how do you get out of a relationship like this? You have to first acknowledge the truth and expose all of your impure motives. Dealing with the truth may destroy your man-made relationship, but you can now build on a new foundation.

As you can continue to get older, you begin to depreciate in value as a young, attractive, beautiful woman. Stretch marks roll across your stomach, sagging eyes from crying, and the tip of your tongue has become exhausted from making excuses for a failed relationship. People play games with their lives from the time they make contact with the opposite sex. They base relationships on misleading information. We put on a beautiful mask and become the character that we created in the midst of our fantasy; usually this character is a seed that have been planted by our own fleshly desires.

There is no such thing as a fairy tale marriage, it just doesn't happen. Some people wish they had found a genie in a bottle that could grant them three wishes: 1. a perfect marriage, 2. financial stability, 3. a dream house. But the catch is that it is all temporary. When the clock strikes twelve, it all it all turns back to ashes. It is so important, as an adult, to sit down and evaluate your life—through God's word—and build it on a biblical foundation that will last a life time. So even in the storms of life—the chaotic moments, the "I hate you moments", the "get out of my life" moments, we had to file bankruptcy moments, and "I lost my job" moments—our relationships will stand as we become one with Christ, sustaining forever.

Now, someone is thinking about a couple that may know that is playing house. Can you help them? Yes, by telling them the truth. Even when they know how the story is going to end, men and women will still gamble with their lives everyday. They moving in together, convincing themselves they are going to be together forever. In reality, you both are only wasting time until you find Mr. and Mrs. Right somewhere else.

Lude 3: weak men run when times get hard

Everyday we hear of sad stories where kids have came home and found their mother sitting at the front door with tears running down her face-all because of the man she gave her mind, body, and soul to. She denied her beauty nine months at a time to conceive beautiful children. Then she finds half a page letter; the man expressed that he didn't love her, he couldn't deal with pressure of life and paying bill collectors. He had to say good bye and tell the kids he loved them. They won't quite understand but one day they would reunite. Now, their sobbing mother is faced to deal with reality. She has a heavy burden and a challenge that has been placed on her. She does not have the slightest clue of how to overcome this. She has to put on a strong face to comfort and reassure her kids that they will be okay.

Ok breathe! Let's think for a few minutes. Is this the time to play the blame game? Or look back on what went wrong? What was said? No. Its time to get on your knees and seek Jesus Christ to give you strength, ability, understanding and wisdom. Ask Him to lead and guide your family down the path of righteousness.

Now, talking to the men: your momma didn't teach you to run, your daddy didn't teach you to run. You have chosen to run from a problem you have helped create. At any time, in your decision making, were you concerned about over extending your finances? Or the outcome of having more children than your finances would allow? Real men don't run!

Men that run face a bigger problem ahead that words can not express, even by reading this book.

Let's reflect a moment. You have just taught your sons and daughters to run every time life overwhelms them. Think for a moment about a single woman raising multiple children on one income—she can not do it. She is going to be forced to make some very uncomfortable decisions about life. She is desperately afraid and she needs money to survive. She is going to be forced into bad relationships because of her blind judgment based on her relationship with you. She may engage in sexual activity just to meet the bills. She may be forced to steal from her place of employment. She may be forced to over charge credit cards just to maintain a comfortable life. Or she may just walk away from everything, move into a shelter and put your children in harms way.

Right now, some man is becoming very angry because you think that I am judging you in this book—judging you without knowing the situation or condition of your life. Judging you is not the problem. You being a man and dealing with your responsibilities is the problem. In the back of your mind you are thinking this will never catch up with you. But you are wrong. Some half dressed hooker will convince you to move in, help her out and not to deal with reality. Now, your little babies are at home wondering why their daddy has left them behind. And their mother has been forced to make excuses and tell lies.

Sometimes fear causes the worst to come out of a man. We suppress our problems by covering up our fleshly sinful nature. We run to keep from dealing with the truth. The truth is we can't take care of our family that God has blessed us with, without His help. It's so easy to build a fairy tale family with picket fences, nice cars and a few dollars in the bank account. But it all disappears when we leave God and Jesus Christ out of the equation. We abandon our children and spouse to fend for themselves in a sinful world controlled by demonic influences. Eighteen years later, both parents have failed to communicate Godly skills, understanding, and Kingdom Principles of maintaining a saved life in an unsaved world. Men were made to bring honor, respect, and account-ability to their family—they are to be a role model and a Godly influence. Running from problems has exposes the weak foundation built on lies instead of building on the Word of God.

Divorce is the worst it has been in history. Let's look at some of the signs we refuse to address or iden-tify. We can easily create a financial burden living a lifestyle above a two salary income. We easily create illusions of luxury through charging up credit cards. We play the blame game to fulfill a void of imma-turity instead of building a marriage to glorify God. Selfish men think about only themselves, while real men think about the concerns and welfare of others. Right now in America there are little boys and girls praying for a daddy to come home that do not love them.

Let's identify the word love. Love has to be built on a solid foundation. Love keeps no record of being mistreated, mentally or physically by someone that claims to love them. Love forgives adultery, fornication, and love gives but rarely takes. Love stands the test of time. Love has no limit, it is unconditional. Love is willing to sweep the dust off and start over. Love gives abundant life. Love opens the door for others to be successful. Love never takes vacation until the work and change is done. Love never plays games with the minds and hearts of others. Love is never pretending to love others. Love is blind by what it sees and hears from people they love. Love takes chastise and correction goes on into their golden years to pursue life. Love can lose everything and start over. Now you see and you have been exposed to what real love is. Do you have these qualities? Or do you talk a good game? Once again I say, weak men will run.

By running, you have released a curse that will haunt your children until someone gives their life to Christ. Now let me give you clarity on this curse. Your sons and daughters will always be runners every time life presents a challenge that makes their lives uncomfortable. They will fail in marriages and other relationships. They will also use excuse of dropping their kids off and will abandon the idea of ever staying committed in a relationship when times get hard. Love can never be established in the hearts of your children because you have released a nucleus that may cause generations of hurt, pain, and suffering. Can you overcome this? The answer is yes. But my question to you would be, are you willing to pay the price to get back into the race? You begin by first asking God for forgiveness, then asking your spouse and children for forgiveness. You have to be able to take full responsibility for the downfall and destruction you have caused your family. Brace yourself like a man! You have been created by God to carry the torch of life! A light that will never burn out as long as you stay engaged with God through Jesus Christ. Remind yourself daily, your life belongs to the Lord. I challenge every man who reads this book, to turn back, regroup and build your family on a solid foundation. Or if you chose not to deal with reality, don't be mad when your kids don't show up to your funeral.

Chapter 10

Divorce is not the Answer

Before mankind was ever created, God had one of the most beautiful plans in the universe. His plan: to bring one man and one woman together for eternal life. His purpose was well planned and he set the perfect scene for husband and wife to mature and grow in perfect harmony and unity.

Adam and Eve were the first man and woman created in the universe. God had given Adam his own world created with unlimited fruits of all kinds and animals of all kinds. God gave him the opportunity to name each animal. But something happened that caused them to miss their perfect destiny.

Adam was the first man to ever have a relationship with God; Eve was the first woman to have a relationship with God. Even though it was the perfect opportunity for a perfect world, God allowed something bad to happen in the Garden. He allowed that serpent—called by the name of the Devil—to manipulate, deceive, and influence negative thoughts.

Now just think for a moment, Eve had a great opportunity to have a perfect life. The stage is set. Adam received instructions from God. He followed these instructions and relayed them to his wife—a wife that God created from Adam's rib. Eve was a woman without excuses. She had no negative influence. She did not have a bad marriage, bad courtship, tabloid magazines, talk shows, or a failed community. And yet she still failed by her own evil desires. She influenced her husband to disobey God. By disobeying God, their perfect world was taken from them—and all because of one bad choice.

The Devil will never tell you the consequences for disobeying God—so he is able to influence you with partial truth, but never the whole truth. Now to make the story short, they are both are kicked out of the Garden of Eden and so was Satan. But Adam and Eve were never allowed to separate and go their own ways.

So once again, divorce is not the answer.

We are living in a society where generation after generation is being taught that it is easier to run from a problem than to correct the problem. Living in a world where men, women, boys, and girls have become so comfortable and relaxed with using these two big words: *blame game*. Society has accepted a lifestyle where we are not held accountable or encouraged in taking responsibility for misdirecting wrong information and inappropriate actions.

Now lets get into the core of all this. It's almost a nightmare for a person to accept the truth about their weakness (or lack of knowledge) when making a mistake. Men and women all over the world have become complacent and comfortable with living imbalanced lives. They are not willing to make necessary adjustments to balance the scale of life. A woman's body is used as an incubator to conceive and carry a baby for nine months; but it only starts as a seed.

One of the greatest gifts of mankind is the natural ability to reproduce. So you cannot fix the problem overnight. It would take you being able to accept the truth about your weaknesses and disconnection from Jesus Christ. Ask yourself this question, do you want to be happy? Have you tried to make yourself happy by creating false little gods? Such as expensive cars, jewelry, homes, multiple academic degrees, expensive wardrobes and the luxury of having babies as an accessory...At the end of the day when you are all alone— deep down in your heart— you weep over the void that cannot be filled by those things. Now you have to accept that you have failed yourself. You have failed your family and others who have drawn strength from a person that didn't love themselves. Now you've become a slave to living a life of lies. But there is some good news. It's never too late to fix this problem. It is going to require sacrifice, loyalty, commitment, and totally excluding the words "give up".

Let's identify the first seed that has to be uprooted from your heart, mind, body, and soul. Hurt is a word that has been used to cover up your weak feelings, but it is not the core of your problem. Making decisions based on short term happiness versus long time commitment is your problem (remember there is a process in planting a seed). You must fertilize the ground, water the ground, and make sure proper sunlight is being exposed to it. It is so important to have a healthy developed seed. Men and women have planted seeds in their marriage, children, homes, family members; seeds that have never taken root. So within months the seed will die because they have no life.

It's very important to know that when you plant a seed the roots have to be developed and go deep into the heart and soul of that person. When your marriage is tested, it can weather the greatest storms. For example, financial hardship, foreclosure on the home you have put your life savings into, a mate is involved with outside relationship or becomes ill, death of a child, loss of well paying job—deep roots enables your marriage can weather the storms.

Second question, are you building your marriage to last a lifetime? Flashback to the first time you saw your mate. Was it love or was it lust? Love is a lifetime commitment of nurturing, empowering, and strengthening your spouse. Lust on the other hand, is a sharp turn relationship built on sexual immorality and impure thoughts. So you can go for long term—which is forever, or short term—which lasts a few months.

When taking advice from a person that does not have a relationship with Christ or biblical standards, you are setting yourself up for failure. Someone that has failed over and over again may have a black heart, retaliation, or revenge in their heart. The only seed they can sew is a seed of destruction.

Marriage was created by God to help replenish the beautiful earth with people created in His image. This journey has caused us to derail and lose focus because we have no love, not accepting the responsibility of being truthful.

Words of wisdom:

A marriage can be successful with God and through God. Each person is responsible for laying down their life for the other and the willingness to love unconditionally until they become one with Christ. Starting over can become an expensive part of the journey, not only financially. Discord between parents and children can cause them to acknowledge that love has a price.

I would like to take you on a little journey.

Love that blinds you:

I have created a selfish life, filled with me, myself and I. I refuse to open my eyes to love. I refuse to allow my guard to be dropped. I own the most valuable key in this world to me: and that is the key to my heart and love. Life has paralyzed me from fulfilling everything I have been created to be by God. By listening to failed marriages of family members and couples, I am kept safe from ever loving anybody that could hurt me and steal my soul. It's not an option. It's not a lifestyle for me. It can't happen.

Being lonely by fear:

Fear was created by the Devil and designed to cause you to never trust God. Fear is a state of mind where you are hypnotized by illusions of failure in this world. You have come to grips that love is not an option, instead of accepting the responsibility that you were created by God. In a society where we live in our dreams—and by living in our dreams we are looking for a perfect family, husband, and children—that can only exist in your imagination. Creating a false sense of living and by using the word "perfect", you have become a slave to a world that will never exist in this lifetime.

Derailing to a life of false balance and altering your destiny forever, you have become ruthless, heartless, and unattached. As life and time ticks away, you became unemotional; dating or marrying people that you could never truly love, because they are not perfectionist. Now your heart has dug a deep, deep cave. You have buried the love that you were created to give to others, freezing your emotions in a state of bitterness, anger, suicide, depression, sadness, and the blame game—deep in a place where no one can pull you back to reality but God. Now you have depreciated half of your life, missing out on a wonderful experience and everything that you were created to be part of.

We fail to acknowledge the truth of being created to give love and take love. From the time a mother gives birth and for the next 3 years of baby's life, that baby is going to be smothered in love. Then as the child begins to mature, the love is taken and redirected. And because the baby has become addicted to love, they will search all their life to fill that void. Dealing with this can help you accelerate into the future. Not accepting or dealing with the truth, can create an internal nuclear explosion that will drain the rest of the joy, peace, and happiness that you may have at this time. Making excuses, not accepting the differences between what is real and what is not real doesn't fix the problem—it delays the healing and deliverance that God has created especially for you to enjoy in life.

Hmmm...what happens when husbands and wives make mistakes?:

Your world has been turned upside down. To fix any problem it's going to take time. Time is one of the most valuable assets that you will have as a human being. Let me clarify with these examples: a man or woman that is on death row and has been given a date of execution—time becomes more valuable than all the wealth of the world. Or a man or woman getting a doctor report that cancer will consume their body in three months—time becomes the most valuable asset in their world. Bills, homes, cars, jewelry—all are no longer priority. Only time...*tick tock...*

Love is an addiction:

Most people fail to acknowledge that they only need to be loved. Your mind, body, and soul will shut down without love. Love fuels the energy to live in a world that was created by God. God is love. There are two types of love. Type A: love that is unconditional. God is the creator of unconditional love. Type B: love with conditions—created by the Devil himself. The Devil gave Eve instruction in the Garden of Eden; if she ate from that Tree of Knowledge of Good and Evil, she would become like God. But the Devil failed to inform her that it would jeopardize and costs her a relationship with God.

Men and women, some 6 billion people, search all over the world interacting, dating and marrying the wrong people because they need to be loved. Women work two and three jobs just to take care of a man so they can be loved. Men work day and night around the clock to make women happy who do not love them. A woman will stay in an abusive relationship just to be loved. A 16-year-old girl will crawl out of her parents window in the midnight hour just be loved. A 17-year-old boy will take his parents car, put it in neutral, and push it out of the driveway, so he can go see a young lady just to be loved. Young ladies will go up and down the street exposing parts of their body for attention and to be loved. Two little boys playing in the neighborhood—one would make suggestion to go into the store and steal something just to be loved. An 18-year-old, who is involved in a gang, will take the life of another young man, just to pass initiation and be loved. A young girl would get on the internet and expose precision parts of her body and drive for a couple of hours to be loved. Young men will rob someone's home and intentionally get caught to get affection and attention from his family to be loved. A 16-year-old girl is pregnant by a 21-year-old man just to be loved. And the list goes on, but I just want to let you think for a moment.

Uncovering the Band-Aid 1:

Some of you may say this makes no sense but there is a purpose for this particular interlude. A prostitute uses sex as a marketable product ranging form 25 cents to $10,000 a night. But God never created sex for a business such as this. Sex should never have a price. God created men and women to have a healthy sexual relationship and replenish the earth that He created for mankind. We were created to take care of the land. But now sex has become one of Satan's number one instruments in creating a $10 billion a year industry—and that industry has accelerated divorce rates into the millennium.

Women with low self esteem and no love have used sex to seduce and entice men. Sex has been used as an instrument to control husbands and manipulate them into buying things they cannot afford. Sex has been used as a reward tool instead of glorifying God. Lust babies continue to come into this unsaved world.

Prostitutes can be found in fortune 500 companies all the way to the crack house. But the bottom line is that a whore is a whore, rich or poor, there is no difference and we cannot justify it. Using our bodies as a capital industry and a money making machine is destroying family after family.

Now freeze this moment in time:

There are about a million babies born in prostitution that will never know who their fathers are. Ask yourself what type of influence are you? Do you produce people with good morals and integrity and a love for God? Or do you produce people who are deceivers, manipulators, self centered, and users? Every man and woman falls under one of these categories. So the next time you are faced with decisions—whether you are a doctor, lawyer, senator, or just a regular person, you are accountable for your actions. The last part of uncovering this band aid—to the men and women that pretend to be soccer moms and dads, coaches, teachers, stay at home moms— when the sun goes down your second personality appears. Get on your knees and ask Christ to come in your heart because you are a very sick individual.

Empty minded people make bad choices.

It's so important that we intake godly wisdom, principles, and a godly relationship. Those are the only things to help you in the days of destructions that are ahead. Divorce is not the answer. We sew so many bad seeds throughout our lives. From the time we are three-years-old into adulthood, somewhere on this journey we forget about all the wrong things we have said and done to people. Unfortunately, the Word of God says, whatever we sew we reap. So we are accountable for our actions and deeds.

It's important that you process this part of the chapter—its life changing. So before you leave this world, whether you sew good or bad seeds, you will be faced to live with the consequences. We live in a world where people easily forget about their actions, gestures, refusing to take responsibility for the bad actions. It is so robotic for a human being to play the blame game. We try to rewrite the script for our actions. Unfortunately because of the emptiness of the minds of men and women, we lie and manipulate to get ahead in life.

Now here is an example to be reckoned with: a young lady in her 20s dating an older gentleman. She pretends to be pregnant, hoping to find compassion and that the older man will do the right thing by marrying her. She plans it out perfect, they become married, and then she tells her husband she has lost the baby. Now the marriage has been built on a life that is designed to self destruct. She becomes jealous, outraged, controlling and uses all these tools and tricks the Devil has personally taught her. Now, she has planted a seed that will backfire on her before she leaves this world. Or if a man steals another man's woman, in time someone will steal his woman too. Or even if you lie on a job application to get a job, when you are confronted on it, you will lose your job anyway. Now this is all from sewing from bad seeds.

Uncovering the Band-Aid 2:

A soccer mom during the day and a prostitute at night; women that live two lives without a conscious. They will go to mass on Saturday with no shame. They easily forget about all the bad seeds they are sewing form destroying homes, families and communities. Ten years down the road her husband cheats on her. Unfortunately, she forgot about all the unfaithful and adulterous things she has done in the last ten years up to this point. She becomes angry, hostile, and upset acting as if she has never been unfaithful in the marriage.

The Devil has a way of using you and then kicking you to the curb. Men and women both have a problem reaping what they have sewn in the past. Life is not fair for anyone that plays with the Devil. Selling your body for fun or pleasure is just a game to you but it's real for others. Most women with low self esteem problems and possessed by sexual demons feel emptiness in their lives and they need help.

So, now here is a woman who is faced to deal with reality. Her husband has committed adultery, he's been confronted by her and he begins to use the old trick of the blame game. He tells her she spends too much time with other soccer moms; he acknowledges that she is not the same woman he married over ten years ago. He continues to explain, *"Haven't you noticed our marriage has been dwindling away?"* and she pretends that she doesn't hear him. He continues to raise his voice...screaming at top of his lungs, *"You didn't have time for me, only your career, the kids and your lifestyle. So don't blame me for eating from someone else's table. I did what I had to do. So where do we go from here? Let's deal with the problem!"* She asks for a divorce, he says fine!

Here is a woman that has the opportunity to expose her dirt but because of pride and embarrassment, she refuses to tell him she has been unfaithful for the last ten years. She uses his failure as an opportunity to go unnoticed—a way to escape the marriage.

It's important to understand why I would put this particular interlude in this chapter. Divorcing will not fix this problem! Divorcing will only allow you to use it as an excuse instead of getting the help needed through Jesus Christ. We must come to grips and terms that a marriage built without God will end up a disaster, prolonging the inevitable.

I pray that as you have read this book, it shines the light on places in your life that will help you realign or establish a relationship with Christ. This is only a tool to assist you with the Word of God. May God's blessings of peace, love, and unity find you.

To be continued...in volume 2 in 2010

CPSIA information can be obtained at www.ICGtesting.com
Printed in the USA
BVOW02s0958111013

333514BV00001B/4/P

9 781607 916468